Feb., 2017

FR Dempsey,
I'm looking forward to
meeting you.

THE ART OF
AFFIRMATION

Robert Furey

D0111689

Paulist Press
New York/Mahwah, NJ

Scripture quotations contained herein are from the New Revised Standard Version: Catholic Edition, Copyright © 1989 and 1993, by the Division of Christian Education of the National Council of the Churches of Christ in the United States of America. Used by permission. All rights reserved.

Cover design by Cynthia Dunne

Library of Congress Cataloging-in-Publication Data

Furey, Robert J.
    The art of affirmation / Robert Furey.
        p. cm.—(IlluminationBooks)
    ISBN 0-8091-4432-8 (alk. paper)
    1. Encouragement—Religious aspects—Christianity. I. Title.
    BV4647.E53F87 2007
    241′.4—dc22

                                              2006034281

Published by Paulist Press
997 Macarthur Boulevard
Mahwah, New Jersey 07430

www.paulistpress.com

Printed and bound in the
United States of America

Contents

Introduction

*L*ook for the best in people. Try to find their gifts and virtues, their strengths and abilities. Recognize their potential, the blessings that are there but not yet obvious.

Finding the best in others is an art that can be learned. It begins with a decision to search for treasure in people. Everyone has God-given gifts. Everyone has gold inside them. Some gifts are quite conspicuous. Others take a little more digging to find.

Everyone has remarkable qualities. Once you decide to look for the best in people, you approach them in a positive, hopeful way. This helps create healthy relationships.

Affirmation is the sincere expression of appreciation for a person's remarkable qualities. It is through this recognition and appreciation that these abilities emerge and grow. Affirmation is a universal need. It is essential for human growth and happiness.

Yet there is too little affirmation in our world. We pay a heavy price for this. When the need for affirmation goes unfulfilled, people fall short of becoming what they were meant to be.

There are reasons for the shortage of affirmation. There are, however, two primary obstacles that block the expression of appreciation and encouragement. First, many people fail to recognize the need for and the power of affirmation. They consider it a nicety when it is, in fact, a necessity. Second, too many of us simply do not know *how* to affirm. Maybe we have not experienced enough of it. Or maybe we have not practiced it enough to develop a style of affirmation that we're comfortable with. In short, we lack confidence in our abilities to affirm. Without this confidence—coupled with the belief that it's just not that important—we tend *not* to affirm.

The good news is we can *learn* the art of affirmation. We can begin with the basics and keep learning all the days of our lives. Affirmation is a beautiful art. Students in this art may become teachers, but they will always remain students. Even the best have the opportunity to keep getting better.

Finding the best in people—and effectively expressing your appreciation for their gifts—is a talent that improves with practice. With the proper guidance, you will get better at it as you go. At first you may only see the most visible gifts. But if you keep looking, you get better at identifying the blessings that often go unnoticed, the emerging, or yet to emerge, abilities that are easily missed. The more you look, the more you find.

As you get better at seeing people's special gifts, the world becomes more beautiful. You see more and more of the valuable qualities that people offer. Your journey in life becomes more scenic when you recognize the beauty in people.

Seeing the best in people, however, need not blind you to their faults. This too is an important skill. I remember my grandfather making a point of this. He said there were people I needed to be careful with. He called them "bad eggs." Whenever he thought he saw such an individual, he would point his finger and say, "Stay away from *that* guy!"

But even the bad eggs have good traits. And often the bad eggs turn into very good people. It's easier to help people improve on their faults when you can see their strengths. You feel more inclined to cheer for folks when you recognize their potential. If you allow yourself to see the best in people, you tend to feel connected to them.

It's easier to love as you become aware of all there is to love. It's easier to believe in God when you see and appreciate his handiwork.

Look for the best in people. Take the scenic route through life.

CHAPTER ONE
Finding the Best in People

W*e all need affirmation. It's a need that begins early and continues throughout life. We need to hear that who we are and what we can do are valued by others.*

Affirmation is the sincere expression of appreciation for someone's gifts, virtues, or special qualities. It's the reassurance that one has something special to offer. Through affirmation, one human being recognizes and acknowledges the good in another. Affirmation is a message that says, "I appreciate you."

There are small affirmations ("You make a great cheesecake") and larger ones ("You bring out the best in people"). You can affirm a particular gift ("I love how you play the piano"), or someone's entire being ("I'm glad you're part of my life").

Affirmation can be written or spoken. There's also the silent kind that often gets missed. Affirmation is the look of joy on a good teacher's face when a student asks an exciting question. You can affirm someone by listening carefully to him or simply patting him on the back.

The need for affirmation is universal. We all need to know we are valued. The need can be quite strong. Still, it can be virtually invisible. We don't change colors when this need intensifies. And, for a variety of reasons, we seldom ask for affirmation.

Those fortunate enough to live in the presence of affirming people are more likely to get this need met. This, consequently, is one of the most important recommendations I can make: in order to be as healthy and happy as you can be, you must find people willing to affirm. My concern, however, is that we do not affirm each other enough. Finding a circle of affirming souls is not always easy. We live in a time where there is a shortage of affirmation. We have failed to recognize the importance and power of feeling appreciated.

I once believed that successful people didn't need affirmation. I just thought there were some individuals who already knew how valued they were and thus didn't need to hear it. I know now this isn't true. Over the years I've met many accomplished people who yearn to know that they are appreciated. The lesson is simple: *we all need affirmation.*

We need it because inside us all there exist certain self-doubts. We want to know: Do I have anything worthwhile to contribute? No matter how successful we may become, there's always a bit of uncertainty. We can never completely overcome this by ourselves. From time to time we need the reassurance of others.

This reassurance brings a certain peace. The restlessness of doubt settles when someone points to our gifts. This may be the first time that gift is noticed, or it may be a much needed reminder of a talent you tend to overlook. An affirmation is a message that says, "You have been blessed. I hope you use this blessing well."

Just as we need to *be* affirmed, we need *to* affirm. I don't think it's a coincidence that the happiest people I have ever known have been affirming souls. We come into this world with a desire to help others become all they can be. When we live this calling, we find our lives have meaning and purpose.

We too often fall short here. We don't encourage as much as we could. When we recognize the beauty in others, we tend to keep it to ourselves. We fear that something unfortunate might occur if we let ourselves be moved by the special qualities of another.

There are many reasons for the shortage of encouragement. Some don't realize the importance of affirmation. Even when they recognize their own such needs, they assume they are unique. They don't understand that everyone has these same needs.

Then there is envy. This is the feeling that seems to say, "It's hard for me to congratulate you for having something I lack. Something I really wish I had."

The feeling of envy affected me for a long time. I have little musical and no artistic abilities. I would have loved being gifted in either of those areas. I think I would have traded any of my talents for either of those two.

As a result, I found it very difficult to admire anyone with artistic or musical skills. It hurt to tell someone how well he painted or how beautifully she played. It felt as if I was rubbing salt into my own wounds. I wanted to admire them, but envy kept getting in the way.

Besides the ignorance and the envy, there's an unfortunate myth about the relationship between affirmation and arrogance. According to this misconception, if I acknowledge your positive traits, I will contribute to your conceit, grandiosity, and narcissism. In other words, the human ego is so prone to extremes that encouragement is likely to make someone feel superior. This myth has killed many kind words.

Here lies an interesting twist: real affirmation does not typically lead to inflated egos. In fact, it more often produces *humility*. Affirmation is an expression of gratitude. Where there is gratitude there is humility. Good affirmation guides us to feel grateful for what we have been given.

Affirmation takes courage. In many circles, encouraging words are not the norm. Many families, classrooms, and work settings lack affirming role models. In such settings, it may take some gumption to tell someone how wonderful he is or that he is doing a good job. Others fear that they'll feel embarrassed or that the person will misinterpret their good words. Especially for those who have not seen the power of affirmation, it can take courage to get started.

Affirmation is an art. But it cannot be learned in three easy steps…or a thousand easy steps, for that matter. All who practice this art bring their own style to the process. Those who affirm well tend to possess certain qualities; however, these skills can be learned and, with practice, anyone can grow in this art.

To grow in the art of affirmation one must also develop ancillary skills that add to the impact of encouragement. One such skill is constructive criticism. The best teachers, coaches, and bosses have a gift for balancing affirmation with constructive criticism.

I like the line from the movie *Camelot* that states: "The uglier the truth, the truer the friend that tells you." In order for affirmation to be fully received, it must be believed. A friend true enough to challenge you becomes believable. This kind of relationship sets the stage for the most moving forms of affirmation. *The art of affirmation is far more than just saying a lot of nice things.* Effective affirmation involves identifying someone's strengths, or potential strengths, and communicating this in an effective way. In order to affirm well you must establish credibility. In short, you earn the right to affirm.

No one, for instance, ever really feels affirmed by a people-pleaser. People-pleasers are motivated by their insecurities. They focus on seeking approval. Toward this end, they will flatter and say what they think others want to hear. Their encouragement is not an expression of appreciation; rather it is an expression of their own fears. Eventually people come to feel this and the power of their words, if there ever was any, wears off.

A middle-aged woman who returned to college not long ago told me about her art teacher. She said, with a shrug, "He told me I have talent. But he tells *everyone* they have talent." Perhaps this professor did, in fact, see talent in everyone. But this particular student didn't feel affirmed. She didn't feel sincerity in his words.

This is one of the fundamental qualities of authentic affirmation—*it must be sincere*. Don't tell the pastor how much you enjoyed his sermon if you slept through it. Don't flatter and try to pass it off as affirmation. You could compliment anything—even someone's shoelaces. But instead, look for qualities, large or small, that strike you as remarkable. Affirmation must be sincere if it is to have power. Sincerity has a sound that people recognize. So does insincerity.

The Eye

Sincerity and courage are fundamental to the practice of effective affirmation. It is also essential that we understand the depth of the human need for affirmation. Affirmation is how we nurture each other's God-given talents. Through this recognition and appreciation of gifts, we help each other become what God intended us to be.

The art of affirmation is more than a set of skills. It must become a lifestyle, a lifestyle that begins with a decision and a commitment to look for the best in others. It is not always easy to learn this art. There are reasons people who want to see the best in others cannot. Still, the hope of finding human goodness never dies. It is a drive too resilient to be destroyed.

A primary reason there is not more affirmation in our world is that so few people have learned this art. People who would like to be more affirming don't know where to start, or feel discouraged when their attempts to encourage fall short.

Affirmation begins with the *desire* to affirm. We come into the world wanting to participate in the growth of others. As children, one of our first behaviors is to clap when someone does something worth clapping for. It is quite natural for us to applaud each other's efforts.

This desire to encourage grows stronger for those who come to understand the human need for encouragement. In a context that minimizes its worth, affirmation may appear insignificant. In such a setting it may hardly seem worth the effort to learn how to affirm. In an environment that recognizes its value, however, the appreciation of another's gifts is more likely to become a lifestyle.

You must work to develop an eye for recognizing what people have to offer. Some seem blessed with a special ability for this. Others have to work a little harder to develop it. But *everyone* can improve. Look for qualities to admire. Everyone has them. The more you look for them, the more you will find them.

In order to affirm someone, you need to *see* his or her gifts. This takes effort. But with practice, it becomes easier. Sometimes a person's finest qualities are subtle, or even hidden.

Then there are those who are so convinced that they have nothing worthwhile to offer that they make little effort to show any of their positives. I once worked in residential treatment programs for seriously troubled adolescents. Many of these kids had become convinced that they were awful creatures incapable of contributing anything useful. They lived with the despair that comes from believing they have nothing of value to offer anyone. As such, they didn't want anyone getting close to them. Keeping people at a distance allowed them some hope of concealing all their perceived flaws. In order to preserve this distance, many of them became quite good at making themselves unlikable.

This distance made it difficult for anyone to see the goodness that had always been there, the goodness that even they didn't realize existed.

When a person, young or old, is convinced that he is inadequate, it can be tremendously healing to encounter someone who has an eye for his gifts—someone who can see past the defenses and recognize the beauty in someone who cannot see it in himself. Sometimes another person has to point to your blessings before you can see them yourself.

But, again, affirmation must be sincere. Many times I saw well-intentioned staff members try to offer praise to one of the kids only to be repaid with scorn. The kids just didn't want to hear it. There were several reasons for this. Perhaps the most common mistake was insincerity. Telling someone you don't know very well that she is wonderful may not be convincing, especially with those who are already reluctant to believe they have anything to be proud of. Consequently, the kids might react as anyone would who felt lied to.

Eventually I learned that when the time was finally right, there was at least one particular affirmation that they were likely to accept. A particular positive quality that they considered possible. So, for many of these young people, my first affirmation to them was, *"You are a survivor!"* It was both the truth and something honorable they could recognize in themselves. If I could get them to accept this first affirmation, their door inched open.

In order to develop an eye for people's talents, it helps to believe these qualities exist. It's not a question of whether or not someone *has* gifts—everyone does. The real questions are: "What are this person's special abilities?" and "How can I point to them in an effective way?"

Developing the ability to recognize strengths can take time and effort. It can be like looking for stars at night. At first, the sky may appear completely dark but if you look closely enough, you will find your first star. Then you find a second. Soon you see so many you can't understand how you missed them all in the first place.

Looking for the best in others is a choice; it's a decision that anyone can make. There's little risk at this point. It's a relatively safe beginning. This is not a decision to change your behavior. It's not a commitment to leave any of your comfort zones. It's a small, but crucial, first step.

If you can accept that everyone has gifts, finding them becomes easier. It's no longer a matter of *"Are they there?"* With the belief that we are all somehow blessed, the question becomes simply, *"Where are they?"*

The decision to deliberately look for what is special in others is, in many ways, a small step. It can, however, be the beginning of an extraordinary change. With the commitment to see the best in others, the world gets brighter. You will see more virtue and talent, potential and triumph. You will encounter reasons for hope and gratitude. Even if you never move any farther in your efforts to learn the art of affirmation, you will be better for having made this step.

Some people stay in this place for a while. They have, or develop, the ability to see the extraordinary in those around them. They may feel confused as to what to do with what they see. They may be weighed down by a belief that affirmation is manipulation or, perhaps, a sign of weakness. Or maybe they would like to express their appreciation of what they see, but lack faith in their ability to do so honestly and effectively. For any number of reasons, one might see the beauty but not know what to do with it.

You must first learn to *recognize human strengths*. This ability improves with practice. It's a simple formula: *the more you look, the more you see*. We have an innate ability to see the good in people. We also have the ability to nurture and develop this skill throughout our lives.

This step requires effort. It may involve a change in your thinking. Consciously looking for positives in people may be new or something you haven't done in a while. As with any change, it can take time to digest and process. Finding the best in people can take patience. Give yourself that time. Look and keep looking. The stars will begin to appear.

The Heart

The art of affirmation begins with a recognition of the importance of affirmation. From there it moves to developing an eye for the gifts of others. Each of these states has its challenges and rewards. And while these steps may reflect significant changes in a person, the changes are still quite private. Things are brewing: a small earthquake may be erupting inside, but there may not yet be any visible signs of change.

This begins to change when feelings get involved. Developing an eye for people's capabilities is an essential start. Then you must let yourself be moved by what you see. The most powerful affirmation contains feeling. Affirmation is an expression of appreciation. As such, it is an expression of emotion. In order to affirm well, you have to let your heart speak. You must let yourself be touched by the blessings of others.

When I was a Cub Scout I made a potholder for my grandmother. From her reaction to this small gift you would have thought I had parted the Red Sea! She couldn't say enough about it. To her, it was far more than a flawed product of arts and crafts class, it was symbolic of something.

Actually, I didn't think the potholder was all that good. But in it she saw the things that grandmothers see. She let herself be moved by what she saw. And here I am, all these years later, writing about it.

In order to affirm well, you have to let yourself see things in the way that grandparents see. Look for the special qualities in people and let yourself be moved by what you see. Develop the eye. Free the heart.

Those most proficient in the art of affirmation can see not only *actual* strengths, they can recognize *potential* gifts. They can see what may be. They appreciate the early signs that suggest someone may have what it takes to be a good artist, mathematician, or swimmer. Good affirmers see abilities before others do.

This is important because it is in its earliest stages of development that a talent is most fragile. Its survival, at this point, may depend on someone's honestly stating, "You could be good at this!" Little affirmations can change lives. They can put someone on the path where he or she belongs. It's sad to think how many people's gifts have gone unopened because no one was there to notice and confirm them when they were small and frail.

Just as good affirmers appreciate potential, they also admire effort. Effort, of course, is a fundamental ingredient in achievement. It is also essential to the development of character. A good affirmer can admire effort even when it is not attached to great ability. A good teacher can appreciate a child's efforts in art class even though the student may not be a great artist. Effort is itself a talent, a talent that deserves to be recognized and appreciated.

Indeed, there's something particularly noble about someone who continues to try in spite of limitations. It's the less-than-athletic parent who tries to help her son play soccer. Or the fellow who signs up to help his church with fundraising even though he lacks the appropriate experience or confidence. You have to admire such people.

Affirmation is not only about strengths. It can be about recognizing how people live with their weaknesses. There's a special place in heaven for those who do their best in areas where they have not been blessed with a great deal of talent.

A good affirmer is someone who roots for people. They hear a calling to help people become what they were meant to be. One skilled in the art of affirmation rejoices in another's efforts and successes.

It is the emotion that communicates sincerity. Whether it be the excitement in your voice or the tears in your eyes, the feeling makes it *real*. Small affirmations may be accompanied by a smile or a pat on the shoulder. Larger affirmations may be conveyed with a cheer and a dance. The emotion reveals that you have been genuinely moved by what you've seen.

As simple as this may sound, it can present problems for a lot of us. Many of us are reluctant to express our feelings. We can be uncomfortable with the expression of emotion. Some people worry that revealing their feelings could get out of control and that it's better to keep them tightly in check. There are others who keep their emotions repressed and have no idea why. They were taught to hide their feelings and have been obedient to this rule—even though they don't understand it. They are simply doing what they were taught to do. (Perhaps by someone who didn't understand the rule either, but who did what he or she was taught.)

Genuine affirmation requires that you allow yourself to feel. You have to see and appreciate the gifts in others. But if you really want to be good at the art of affirmation, you have to *love* the gifts in others. You must recognize your part in the birth and life of these gifts. You need to feel the gratitude for the honor of being a part of this birth. As these feelings deepen, your ability to affirm will grow.

This is a process, one that goes through stages. You may have to look a while before you become good at finding the best in others. Once you can recognize strengths, it may take time before you allow yourself to feel the emotions that come with these discoveries. Then it may be a little longer—and perhaps require some coaching—before you begin to communicate both what you see and how you feel.

A cold heart envies. A warm heart affirms. A cold heart can warm. The warmth increases as you look for the best in others and allow yourself to be moved by what you see.

Admiration

H. L. Mencken wrote, "A teacher is one who, in his youth, admired teachers." Affirmation is how we help others become what they were meant to be. But there is another side to this. As Mencken suggests, the process of affirmation helps us become the people *we* were meant to be.

Admiration summarizes the first phase of affirmation. It's the recognition of strength or virtue. It's the feeling of awe that moves us at the sight or thought of these wonderful qualities.

Admiration reveals something about us. We admire those who have traits we would like to see in ourselves. Qualities such as courage, respect, honesty, patience, generosity, leadership, perseverance, or kindness. Admiration is a form of inspiration. You see the virtue. You let it touch you. You feel grateful, reassured, and somehow, empowered. The people we admire become our own personal heroes. They inspire us to move toward becoming the best we can be.

Those we admire make it easier for us to "hold on" to a faith in human strength and goodness. When we allow ourselves to admire, we become healthier.

Admiration can be practiced without risk. You can admire a statesman or writer who lived a hundred years ago. You can admire your neighbor without telling him or her. These wouldn't involve any risky self-disclosures—you can simply admire from a distance. As such you don't have to worry about how you might come across or how you might be misinterpreted. Admiration is a first step. But an important one.

And, if Mencken is to be believed, admiration is a necessary step in the journey to discover your purpose in life. The qualities you admire most may indeed be the traits you would like to see in yourself.

To learn the art of affirmation you need to free yourself to admire. Look for people with admirable traits. There are more of these individuals than there are stars in the sky. Look at them. Let them touch you. Then be grateful for them.

The world becomes a much brighter place when you let yourself admire others.

CHAPTER TWO
The Unaffirmed
and the Unaffirming

*M*any do not get the affirmation they need. In fact, I've come to believe that the single most common unmet need is the need for affirmation.

Psychiatrist Conrad Baars, in his fine book *Born Only Once: The Miracle of Affirmation*, writes, "Affirmation is at the root of all happy human existence."[1] Obviously we can survive without it—many people do. But without affirmation we will never grow to be all we could be.

One way to understand our need for affirmation is to recognize the damage that occurs when this need is not met. This damage can be severe and lasting. To a point, the damage can be repaired. But the longer the deprivation continues, the more difficult it can be for the scars to heal.

Understanding the consequences of living in a discouraging environment is not simple. First, there are degrees of affirmation. A little may not be enough, but it's better than none. And some people, including children, are amazingly resilient. Even if they've not received many positive words, they can squeeze every ounce of strength from what they've been given.

Consider Kelly. A young adult, Kelly struggles with many of the symptoms of inadequate affirmation. Raised in a safe but unaffirming family, she never developed a healthy confidence in her worth or abilities. She has had few close friends. Yet there is a real goodness to her. She is reliable and hardworking, and she volunteers her time to several good causes. She is a genuinely generous person.

So much of her health, I believe, stems from her relationship with her wonderful Aunt Vicki. Aunt Vicki was a ray of sunshine in Kelly's dark childhood. Two or three times a year, Vicki would visit and bring with her an outpouring of love and affection that Kelly might otherwise not have experienced.

Aunt Vicki would gently squeeze her face and tell her she was beautiful, even on days when she didn't feel beautiful. And Aunt Vicki would emphatically reassure her of her intelligence, even when she didn't feel so smart.

When Aunt Vicki left, so did the affirmation. Kelly, however, knew it was out there and would come back when her aunt visited again. To be sure, Kelly did not receive all the affirmation she needed. But she knew it existed, so she made the most of what little she had received.

There are many people with their own "Aunt Vickies"—people who have not experienced adequate reassurance and encouragement but who nurture memories of people who affirmed their worth. Often it's a special teacher. Sometimes it's a grandparent, neighbor, coach, or Scout leader. Any single soul who affirms well can do a great deal to fill a dark void.

When we speak of someone being unaffirmed, we are measuring in degrees. Some people, like Kelly, have had their need for affirmation partially met, others almost not at all. The extent of the damage—what I will refer to as the *scars*—typically reflects the degree of deprivation. Still, we must keep in mind that some individuals (like Kelly) are able to draw a lot from a little.

The Scars

Those who have not received healthy amounts of affirmation are at a disadvantage. Lacking the support needed to grow to their potential, they accumulate wounds, while other, more appropriately affirmed souls, gather strength.

Inadequately affirmed people can be guarded. They may be quiet and reserved or they may be quite extroverted. In either case, they are reluctant to reveal themselves. They haven't lived in a welcoming world, so they hold back. They may present what psychologists call a *false self*. That is, they create an image of what they believe is acceptable. This image, which is more or less a mask, covers the real self that lies beneath.

Living in an unaffirming context one learns to hide things that are personal. There's a fear of revealing too much. Unaffirmed people are tentative in their relationships. They may bend over backwards to meet other people's needs, but honest self-disclosure is difficult. No one wants to be exposed to what could be an unfriendly world.

Without adequate affirmation we become indecisive. It's hard to put your best foot forward if you're not sure you have a best foot! This is the talented young athlete who can't decide whether or not to go out for the team. Or the very competent adult who can't decide if she should apply for the promotion. These people know what they *want;* they're just not confident they have the *abilities* to move toward their goals. Further, they may be uncertain whether they could survive the possible failure. As they sit and try to decide, opportunities come—and go.

Without encouragement, people struggle to develop initiative. First steps—the most frightening ones—are painful. Whether it's asking someone for a date or starting a new project at work, making the move from passive to active can be an especially difficult transition. It's hard to move boldly forward when one hasn't had enough healthy supporters.

When we receive adequate affirmation it takes root. Good affirmation has a way of sticking with us. Our "cheerleaders" move inside us. We then have affirming memories we can retrieve and hold. These recollections strengthen and energize. They provide a supply of support and motivation that can sustain us when we begin to doubt ourselves. Affirmation, if we let it, can stay with us throughout our lives.

I sometimes ask my clients to write a list of all the affirmations they've received. Since few people have a conscious list prepared, it usually takes a while to get the list rolling. Once it gets started, however, they are often surprised at the memories that surface. Sometimes we have to make a deliberate effort to find them, but these memories are amazingly resilient. They may be lost, but they can be found.

It's wonderful to watch people reconnect with an old memory of someone taking the time to tell them how good or talented they are. These recollections usually begin with a smile, a slight shake of the head, and a look in the eye that indicates that their entire being is now back in time. Then comes the announcement: "I remember Mrs. Jackson in second grade…" or "I can just see my old college professor Dr. Miller telling me…" These memories are more than details; they are stories that come *alive* and are *meant to stay alive*.

Those who do not have a sufficient collection of such memories experience a certain loneliness. Affirming people come with us as we travel through life. We may ignore them, take them for granted, or refuse to appreciate them (and thus reduce their contribution to our lives), but they are there. Unaffirmed people, on the other hand, don't have enough Aunt Vickies, Mrs. Jacksons, or Dr.

Millers. Without these people tucked safely somewhere inside us, we are vulnerable to feeling lonely. We would feel alone as we made the big presentation at work or submitted the application for a new job. We would feel alone with our failures, and even our successes. Without a healthy history of support and encouragement, we are apt to feel uncomfortably alone whenever we begin to leave one of our comfort zones. It may feel safe to think and plan our journey into uncharted waters. These dreams may be alluring and invigorating. But when it comes time to leave shore, the loneliness and fear set in.

Nearly everyone feels some level of anxiety when they step beyond their safety zones. Those who have been affirmed, however, feel accompanied on their journey. They travel with everyone who ever reminded them that they have the resources to survive and grow. They carry with them everyone who ever reassured them that they are valuable and capable of making important contributions. If they keep their memories alive, the people who once strengthened them can continue to empower them.

Those without sufficient supplies of affirmation lack this essential source of strength. They look for safe places to live—and sometimes hide. Dreaming may come easily, indeed they may spend a great deal of time in fantasy. But to move beyond the relatively safe and predictable is unsettling. Not only might they lack the *confidence*, but also the *faith* that there are individuals who are willing to help them. When we move out of the old and into the new, it helps to have someone cheering for us. Sometimes these cheerleaders have to be people from our past, people who cheered for us so well that their memories continue to motivate and comfort.

Sometime early in life, usually by early adulthood, we make an important decision. It's a decision about people. We decide how supportive we can expect them to be. If our experience leads us to conclude that people can—and often will—be encouraging, we approach life with the hope that what we have to offer will be welcomed. We hope because there is reason to hope. We've seen the side of people that appreciates our efforts and our gifts. This fuels our faith in humanity and motivates us to learn and grow.

If, however, we have not received enough genuine affirmation, we may reach an entirely different conclusion. The world feels less inviting. No one seems eager to appreciate our next step. We then assume that our audiences will inevitably be uninterested or even hostile. Instead of revealing what is real and unique about ourselves, we show only what is safe.

This need for safety can lead to a life trapped in comfort zones. In a comfort zone there may be little applause, and even less fulfillment, but there is minimal fear of the unknown. In this land of comfort, one lives safe and unchallenged. Talents go undeveloped and passion dies young. Here life remains largely unexplored: few risks, few rewards. You don't start to climb mountains until you *believe* you *can* climb mountains. It is through the encouragement of others that we come to believe.

The unaffirmed are less likely to take even reasonable risks. They are reluctant to explore the possible.

They're not convinced that new contexts could give rise to new abilities. Again, experience has not assured them that ours is a welcoming world. Nor has it given them assurances that they can survive the challenges life may throw at them. So they *avoid* challenges. Preferring to live and work in places that are easy to control, they abandon their potential in the pursuit of security.

There is, however, a twist here. While unaffirmed people shy away from appropriate risks, many are attracted to *un*reasonable ones. Someone starved for appreciation may go to dangerous lengths to gain much-needed attention. I once treated a seventeen-year-old named Kevin who was brought to a mental health clinic because of self-destructive behaviors. Specifically, he repeatedly injured himself "car surfing." He would stand on top of a car while his friends drove, reportedly, up to forty "or so" miles per hour. In spite of a growing number of brutal falls, Kevin wouldn't stop doing this.

When I first met him, his arms were heavily bandaged. He had cuts on his face and hands. It became clear that Kevin believed that "car surfing" was his one and only talent. Actually, he was so desperate to have someone, anyone, appreciate something—anything—about him, that he willingly risked his life in order to impress his so-called friends.

Unaffirmed individuals may compromise their values and even risk their lives for some indication that they have something valuable to offer. If the need for affirmation is frustrated long enough, it may go underground. But it *never* goes away. Even when someone stops believing they will ever be affirmed, the need continues, but it may exist outside of their awareness. They then may engage in a wide variety of attention-seeking behaviors without ever understanding *why*. They don't recognize that underneath it all is the burning desire to know that they are appreciated.

Those who are unaffirmed may also use their sexuality in this way. A person's first desire is to be affirmed while maintaining his or her values. If this does not seem possible, compromises in one's moral code are often made. But even if this is successful and affirmation comes their way, it does so accompanied by guilt. They may gain attention and flattery from others, but lose respect for themselves.

I've treated many men and women who use sex to find affirmation. Most have used a great deal of self-deception in an effort to make this work. If only briefly, they convince themselves that their sexual encounters are proof of how desirable they are. This need to please can, of course, make them quite vulnerable to manipulation.

Charlene, a former client, made this point quite well. She was court-ordered to treatment after an arrest for possession of cocaine. Charlene was a dancer at a large "men's club." She made a good deal of money and had no intention of changing careers.

She told me that she "had" to do cocaine in order to keep her job. When she noticed my puzzled look she added, in a slightly impatient tone, "Look, Doc, it's like this: guys come to watch me dance. But more than that, they want me to *like* them. I have to smile, laugh with them, and act like I really *do* like them. Most of them are gross. So in order to act like I like them, I have to be high."

Charlene pretended to affirm needy men, men who were so needy that they refused to see the insincerity of her pseudo-affirmation. With enough alcohol, they could perhaps convince themselves it *was* real. Then there was Charlene herself, who also practiced self-deception. With enough cocaine, she could convince herself that men cared for her. Her romantic relationships were short-lived. These men could seduce but not affirm. She needed her drugs to help her to lie and to believe in other people's lies. She had no real love or affirmation in her life.

I don't know what happened to Charlene. Shortly after she began to reevaluate her life and rethink some of her decisions, she disappeared. No one seemed worried. I never saw her again.

Unaffirmed people often fall into addictions. Addictions are one way to meet needs you can't name or don't know how to deal with. An addict tries to get all his or her needs met through a select group of sources. Some use alcohol. Others use gambling or eating or spending. There are many unaffirmed souls among the ranks of the addicted.

Possible Consequences of Inadequate Affirmation

- Low Self-Esteem
- Lack of Initiative

- Fearfulness
- Interpersonally Distant
- A False Self
- People-Pleasing/Approval-Seeking
- Addictions
- Lack of Spontaneity
- Undeveloped Talents
- Overly Sensitive
- Toxic Memories
- Fear of Asking for Help

The frustrated need for affirmation is an unexplored condition. Most people who suffer with this cannot explain what ails them. If they can describe it at all, they may call it depression, anxiety, or some variety of "It's just the way I've always been." Until we more fully appreciate the depth and intensity of the human need for affirmation we will never understand the consequences that develop when this fundamental need goes unmet.

Unaffirmed people sometimes have trouble explaining the impact of certain memories. We typically think of a traumatic memory as one when someone recalls an event where something terrible happened to her or him. In recent years we've learned more and more about how such recollections can affect the human psyche. But there is another, far less recognized and less understood, kind of toxic memory that impacts the unaffirmed: memories of things hoped for that never occurred.

Like traumatic memories, these may be repressed and avoided since they cause pain. They are the memories of when you did your absolute best and no one noticed. Or the time you thought you had finally done enough to hear someone say "Good job," but it never happened. And the times you worked hard to reveal the best in you, and no one seemed to care. Whereas traumatic memories often generate anxiety, these memories continually reproduce the original feelings of disappointment.

We all probably have at least a few of these memories. Some people, unfortunately, have enough of these scenes stored inside them to conclude that ours is an unaffirming world.

The unaffirmed have many wounds. Sometimes these wounds are masked well and carried quietly. Often they leave permanent scars. Yet there *is* hope: human beings have a miraculous ability to heal.

But this leads to a final concern: people who have not experienced adequate affirmation are often reluctant to ask for help. It can be frightening to reach out to what you believe is an unsupportive world. So the need for healing becomes less important than the need for safety.

Thus, for many, the scars that come from being unaffirmed are lasting.

The Unaffirming

We have a need to affirm. We have a need to have an impact on other people in a positive way. Not everyone recognizes this need. And even among those who do, not everyone moves to meet this need. There are different reasons people refuse to encourage others. Often they feel afraid. They fear their kind words will be interpreted in a way that will cause embarrassment. Or perhaps they fear the intimacy that may develop from their affirmation.

There is yet another reason. So often the expression of affirmation is blocked by ignorance. Someone who has not seen it done well, someone who has not had enough opportunity to experience the power of affirmation—this person may be forever reluctant to risk the honest self-disclosure that is affirmation.

Whatever the cause, the decision to keep from affirming others has consequences. It may feel like the safe choice, but it is a destructive one. Destructive not only to all those people who could have been affirmed, but also to the individual who will not allow himself or herself to appreciate the good in others.

Those who will not affirm live at a distance. Both spiritual and emotional health require that we help others become the best they can be. Without an honest effort to appreciate and admire, there will always be a distance between those who are unaffirming and other people.

You may love someone, but without affirming her, you will love her from a distance. You may need someone, but unless you can express to him all the wonderful things you see in him, he may never know he is loved or needed. In order for human beings to really connect, affirmation must be given and received.

Living at a distance has its consequences. It can be a painful existence. It can be lonely, depressing, and confusing. Some people use this pain to motivate them to change in positive ways. Others refuse to change, or never learn how to make the appropriate corrections, and get stuck in this situation. They are unable or unwilling to affirm. Instead of changing for the better, they try to learn to live with the discomfort.

Those who will not affirm look for ways to survive the distance that exists between them and others. They try to find ways to live with the pain this distance produces.

We have a remarkable talent for finding how to avoid difficult realities. Those who are unwilling (or feel unable) to affirm others will rely on a wide variety of defenses to live with this unmet need. Many begin by denying the need. They may convince themselves that people don't need encouragement or, perhaps, that affirmation is a form of coddling that only produces negative consequences. People who think this way may surround themselves only with others who think similarly.

If they cannot deny the need completely, they may try to qualify it. Adults who are uncomfortable with affirmation may accept that *children* require it. They may not acknowledge, however, that adults do. A slightly different version suggests that affirmation may indeed be a real need, and adults may in fact need to be affirmed. But the need is a small one and one must take great care not to overindulge this need. In this case, you may have an employer who is uncomfortable expressing affirming words to his staff. At the same time he can't help but recognize that people love to be affirmed. So he reaches a compromise. He allows himself to express his gratitude for their talents and efforts, but he will only do it at *Christmas*. He then tries to persuade himself that this is more than adequate for all of his employees for the entire year.

This employer tells himself that it would not be healthy to voice such appreciation more often. He may support this mistaken belief by explaining to himself that his employees will become egotistical if they are given any additional sincere, positive feedback. He may also convince himself that if he strengthens their self-confidence, they will all demand raises.

A person who has decided not to affirm is capable of putting together theories to support that position. Still, the need lives on. And when a need is denied, the pain and strain that results is often difficult to understand.

People who will not affirm often live with the feeling that something is missing. In order to avoid this uneasy feeling, they may try to avoid *all* their feelings. Those who will not affirm lack the warmth that is so apparent in affirming people. They may appear to be a little distant or they may present themselves as outright cold and aloof. There are degrees of distance. Unaffirming people experience more loneliness than most, but they may mislabel their condition. They may describe themselves as being frustrated by or disappointed in others. Anger can be a powerful feeling and thus it is often used to mask more vulnerable feelings like hurt, fear, and loneliness.

Those who allow themselves to be vulnerable have a better chance of healing. People who suffer honestly are more likely to find the answers they need. The first image that comes to mind of an unaffirming person might be a mean, abusive Scrooge-like figure. While such personalities *do* exist, they are outnumbered by more normal-looking characters who are more or less aware of their inability to express admiration.

For the most part, unaffirming people know something is missing from their lives, although they may not be completely clear as to what that is. This perceived, though often unexplained, void leaves them feeling unsure. They may see the good in others but lack an understanding of what to *do* with what they see. They would like to applaud, but are prone to envy, which is another uncomfortable feeling. Many unaffirming people are stuck in the rut of constantly comparing themselves with others. They may conclude that *any* affirmation they give someone else is a sign of defeat, as though they were admitting that the other person is better than they are.

While there are those who fight hard to remain unaffirming, this is the minority. Most unaffirming people would love to be more affirming. Not only do they *want* to be affirming, they want to do it *well*. They may root for sports teams, entertainers, and political figures all in an effort to be more affirming. But *real* affirmation is a *lifestyle*. It involves cheering for those whom you are close enough to touch. It means rooting for people because you recognize the human need to give and receive affirmation.

Some people spend their entire lives waiting for permission to begin. They withhold what they need to share. As a result, so much of who they are is *never* revealed.

The pledge to be a more affirming person is seldom seen on any list of New Year's resolutions, but it should be. Becoming a more affirming person is a *realistic* goal. It is a change that can start small and build. In the process, people can significantly improve their lives and the lives of everyone they touch.

Individuals who move from unaffirming to affirming find more enjoyment in life. They experience the freedom of becoming more the person they were meant to be. They eliminate many of the barriers that stand between them and the people in their lives. There is less jealousy and more admiration; less competitiveness and more encouragement. By becoming more affirming, they realize their impact. They come to discover their own significance in others' lives.

As the willingness to encourage develops, relationships improve. Because they now reveal more of themselves, there is less loneliness. Not only do they come out of their shell—or their disguise—they come out with a purpose. They come into their own for the purpose of improving the world, one person at a time.

Those who are reluctant to affirm are less than what they could be. Because we live in a world where we do not affirm as much or as well as we could, we are *all* less than what we could be. This can and must change. We can learn to be more affirming. We can learn to reach out and encourage others.

In the process of becoming more affirming, one becomes happier, healthier, and more connected to other people. Indeed, becoming more affirming is often the simplest and most direct path to greater health and happiness.

CHAPTER THREE

Free to Affirm

*I*f we are afraid to affirm others, we can create any one of a thousand reasons to avoid it. We can insist that it will only make someone conceited or that he or she doesn't need it anyway. We can convince ourselves that praising someone's efforts will inevitably appear insincere and manipulative. Another favorite excuse is to persuade ourselves that affirmation only makes people uncomfortable and that we should spare them (and us) this discomfort. None of these are necessarily true, but if we are anxious enough, we can make them sound believable to ourselves.

Then there are the fears. Many men, for example, believe that affirmation is a feminine gesture. Consequently, many children grow up unaffirmed by their fathers. The neglect produces painful wounds. And the tragic myth that affirmation is somehow unmanly can continue through generations.

There is, however, a more valid fear, one that must be recognized and faced in order to free ourselves to affirm. As we cannot control how someone will react, we must accept that even the kindest words may not be received as such. There are those who become unsettled when anyone suggests they have something valuable to contribute. Often this unsettledness is rooted in feelings of inadequacy. To those convinced they have little or nothing worth affirming, affirmation may sound insincere. Furthermore, through affirmation people become closer. Those who fear this closeness will resist what affirmation comes their way. This resistance may be subtle or quite direct.

In chapter six we will deal with how people receive affirmation. For now, suffice it to say that if affirmation were always received well, there would be more of it. But, as we said, it's not always taken well. And because affirmation is not always accepted gratefully or graciously, it sometimes requires courage, patience, and perseverance.

People who are uncomfortable being affirmed use a number of techniques to prevent it. Many of these individuals are unaware of why they use such techniques, or even that they are using them at all. Most of these strategies attempt to send the same message: "Don't do that again!"

If you tell them you liked their presentation, they may appear shocked and say something like, "Oh come on! You liked *that?*" Then, rather than having a *good* feeling, you feel *criticized*. Or they may simply send a nonverbal message that makes it clear that what you just said made them feel uneasy. Exchanges such as these decrease the likelihood that they will have to deal with any more of your praise. They may also cause you to question the value of affirmation in general.

Learning the art of affirmation involves getting bruised now and then. Affirmation fills a fundamental human need. Still, not everyone knows *how* to receive it. Although this may feel discouraging to you, remember this: *those who refuse your encouragement are often the people who need it most.*

I once worked for a large mental health center that had some serious staff morale problems. Assorted attempts were made to correct the situation, but nothing seemed to help. There were special staff meetings, a staff retreat, a suggestion box, even a Christmas bonus. Still, it was clear something was missing.

Then, Sally, a young intern, arrived. Intuitive enough to quickly gauge the situation, Sally offered what seemed to be a ridiculous remedy. She suggested we write "affirmation notes" to each other and post them on the bulletin board in the staff lounge. She made colorful slips of paper with creative little designs. She then cordoned off a section of the bulletin board specifically for the notes.

Sally said we should write affirmations to each other as the opportunities presented themselves. She wanted us to write the affirmation, fold the paper, and write the person's name on the outside before putting it on the board.

There was, to say the very least, resistance. When she presented the idea, you could see the eyes rolling heavenward. It seemed like a trite exercise. We had *real* problems and writing niceties on little pieces of paper didn't seem powerful enough to correct the situation. The project began without much support or enthusiasm.

The first few days saw little activity on the board. In fact, I'm pretty sure that the first notes were written by one person: the intern. Then it happened: more notes. Then more. You could see people looking hard at the board as they passed, hoping to find their names on a note. It was almost magical. Most of the notes were signed, but not all. People could affirm without revealing themselves. Some people needed to start this way.

As the staff came to feel the power of affirmation, they became more affirming. Even those who most resisted the idea came around. It became clear that their resistance was based in the denial of an important need. If you don't believe the world will affirm you, you may try to deny your need for it. Once you feel the power of affirmation, you are reminded how much you, and everyone else, requires it.

After a couple of weeks, staff members were posting the affirmation notes in their offices. Some were carrying them in their wallets. We had become a group of people who were teaching each other how to affirm. We were learning how to appreciate each other.

Gradually it became clear how we had gone wrong. In trying to correct our troubled situation we focused on our mistakes. We looked at our flaws, faults, bad decisions, and regrets. While there is a time to study all these things, we had abandoned the search for what we were good at. It wasn't until we balanced ourselves by looking at all the good that we became unstuck and started growing again.

To learn the art of affirmation it helps to remember the moments in your life when you were affirmed well. Recall the scenes, sit with the memories. Feel the emotions that come with it. Let yourself experience the power of affirmation.

You may feel an impulse to let go of these memories too quickly. While these recollections are often quite beautiful, they may come with a touch of sadness or grief. Recognizing what you once had may remind you of what you have lost. Good affirming memories may soften and sadden you. Not everyone is immediately comfortable with this.

Then there are those who are uneasy with feelings of gratitude. Gratitude is fundamental to the art of affirmation. *First*, affirmation is an expression of gratitude. In order to master this art you must allow yourself to feel grateful, not only for what you've been given, *but for what others have been given*. An affirmation is a communication that says, in effect, "I am grateful for your wonderful music abilities," or "I appreciate your gift of teaching." When you can feel grateful for another person's blessing, you will have the sincerity needed to affirm effectively. With this gratitude, you speak from the heart. Words spoken from the heart are of course the most sincere.

Second, affirmation *produces* gratitude. Receiving sincere affirmation leaves one feeling thankful. Thankful for the gift that is being recognized and thankful for the soul who is taking the time and effort to recognize it. Memories of affirmation stir gratitude.

Those who are reluctant to feel gratitude will resist affirmation. They will avoid giving it and they will resist receiving it. Gratitude can be a powerful feeling. It has an energy that can be difficult to harness. It can transform someone from a stoic, emotionally repressed control-freak into a joyful, vibrant, giving individual. Its potential power is so great it can be frightening! Gratitude moves people. It is welcomed only by those willing to be moved.

If you can allow yourself to feel gratitude, it will be easier to recall times when people noticed your special qualities or the occasions when someone saw a strength in you that you didn't see in yourself. Recall these scenes, and let yourself stay with them for a time, and the power of affirmation will emerge.

One of the healthiest things you can do for yourself is to remember your special moments of affirmation—those moments when someone said something so encouraging that you can still feel it. Good affirmation can last a lifetime. Sometimes it's not so much what was said or how it was said. At times, the most important dimension is *who said it*. There are some individuals who, by virtue of who they are or their position, have a special way of getting your attention and making their words believable.

I learned this early on. I spent my youth playing sports. I was on all the teams. When the games ended, it was always nice to hear compliments from your own team's parents. At the same time, though, you *expected* good words from them (no matter how badly you played). And it was great to hear encouragement from your coach. But when one of the parents from the *other* team took the time to affirm you, it really moved you. To hear one of the other team's parents say something like, "Hey, number eight, nice hustle!" had a special power to it. They weren't obliged to pat you on the back. Thus there was something especially sincere and memorable about it.

Affirmation *connects* people. An affirmed person feels *included*. One who affirms is also more likely to feel included in the larger community of humankind. Affirmation is an invitation to continue sharing all the special qualities you've been given. It's a communication that says your gifts are valuable and will be welcomed. With enough of these messages, delivered in the right way, you start to believe that you can contribute.

An important dimension of the art of affirmation is knowing when you are in a position to deliver an especially powerful piece of encouragement. When someone values your opinion, you can make a lasting impression. When someone respects your sincerity, you are also in a strong position to affirm. There are occasions when life simply puts you in a time and place where an expression of appreciation for someone's abilities can have a very special impact.

I've had this lesson presented to me repeatedly as well. You must be aware when you are in a position to *influence* someone. These moments often arise unexpectedly and can be easily missed.

Shortly after I finished graduate school, I decided it was time to make my first professional presentation. I submitted a proposal to do a workshop at the annual conference of the Missouri Association for Marriage and Family Therapy. I put a great deal of time and energy into the project and was thrilled when the committee accepted it.

When the conference finally arrived, I was as prepared as I had ever been for anything. I was so well prepared, I thought, that nothing could spoil the day. I was ready for any question, comment, or disaster.

During my time slot there were two other presentations in other rooms. I had visualized an audience of about fifty people and considered the possibility that there might even be more. I had prepared for everything. Except for a very small audience.

When my much-anticipated moment arrived, I found myself staring at an audience of exactly *two*. Two cordial souls who probably felt uncomfortable, but who could not possibly have felt more ill at ease than I did. As I sat there with my pile of handouts and all those empty chairs, it occurred to me that I was at a crossroad. I didn't want to continue with the presentation since I felt foolish, embarrassed, and hurt. But I knew that if I canceled the talk, I might not ever get back into the ring again.

So I threw myself into it. I presented with all the passion I could muster. At one point, I even stood on a chair to make a point. While this may be passionate in front of a large audience, it probably looked ridiculous with an audience you could count on two fingers. It wasn't hard to stay focused on both participants and I tried to answer their questions as best I could.

When our time ran out, they thanked me quite warmly, shook my hand, and left. I was too caught up in my own disappointment to hear what they said to me, but I remember thinking that they seemed like such nice people.

Then I sat for a few minutes alone in that room. I was glad that I had gone ahead with the talk, but I was demoralized. My grandmother used to talk about signs from God. I wondered if this had been a sign that public speaking and adult education were just not for me. I had started the day thinking this would be the first step in an exciting phase of my new career. By dinner time it certainly felt like that dream had ended!

Then came the lesson. A week or so after the conference, the presenters received written evaluations of their presentations. All participants were given the opportunity to provide feedback to the speakers. My tiny audience seized the opportunity. To this day I wish they could know how their words affected me. These two people—one man, one woman— took time to write very affirming responses. They gave examples of what they learned and expressed sincere gratitude for the experience. These two souls were skilled in the art of affirmation. They put energy back in the dream. They both conveyed the same message: "Hang in there. Keep at it."

Neither of them signed the feedback forms. I'm sure my grandmother would have said they were angels. And, really, those who affirm well tend to have an angelic quality to them. Two people, whose names I'll never know, took a few minutes to write notes. Now, over twenty years later, it's still impossible to articulate how important their words have been to me. They helped keep me on course when I was considering safer, less challenging paths. This is the power of affirmation. Although often brief encounters, they can, and often do, influence the course of someone's life.

Affirmation is the encouragement we need to grow, reach, accept challenges, and explore the frightening and new. Through affirmation we help each other accept who we are and who we could be. Affirmation may be your greatest contribution to another human being. But you won't always know how much of a contribution you've made. Some of the people you affirm may only realize its impact years later.

Today, in my talks on affirmation, I typically ask the audience to list all the positives that come from it. It doesn't take long to produce a sizeable list. Items that show up on most lists include improved self-esteem, greater confidence, increased courage, a greater willingness to risk, the development of talents, a clearer sense of self, and a stronger connection between people. In most groups someone is quick to point out that people who receive enough affirmation are happier and more hopeful and they come to see the world as a healthy, safe place where they and their gifts are welcome. Usually someone suggests that people who are adequately affirmed are more likely to be affirming.

In all these sessions, I've never seen a short list. Once the board is filled, I ask the groups to stop for a minute and look at it. After a moment or two of quiet reflection, I ask them, "If affirmation can do all these wonderful things, why isn't there more of it?"

Typically, the room stays quiet for another couple of moments as they absorb the point. Then we spend a little time discussing why people often struggle to express appreciation for others' gifts. But this gives way to the more important question: "What keeps *you* from being more affirming?"

As I have said, two of the most common reasons we avoid affirming others are that (1) we don't recognize the importance of affirmation, and that (2) we don't feel confident in our abilities to do it effectively. There are, however, other reasons. Each of us must look within ourselves to see if there are fears, biases, or other issues that might keep us from contributing more to others.

Finish this sentence as many ways as you can: "I would like to be more affirming but _____." Give it some time and thought. What comes after the "but"? Is there one thing in particular? Or is there a combination of several things? What are the obstacles to your efforts to affirm?

It helps to name these obstacles in your path. It's easier then to find solutions. It's also less difficult to ask for help once you can describe your situation. Furthermore, once you name the forces that limit you, they come into the light and often lose much of their power.

Keep in mind that new behaviors typically produce some anxiety. With affirmation, this obstacle isn't insurmountable. You can start small. You don't have to show up for work tomorrow and praise everyone for every talent they've been given. Instead, you can look for a single opportunity to express your appreciation for someone's gifts. Begin with someone with whom you feel safe. You can start the process as slowly as you like. Build from there.

As you grow in the art of affirmation you become freer. Your fears subside. You become less focused on yourself. Your uncertainty and confusion are no longer the center of your attention. Your focus shifts. You become freer to tend to other people. As this develops, you have more energy available to look for the remarkable features in others. In time, and with practice, affirmation comes to feel more and more natural.

It feels natural because it *is* natural. We are affirming creatures by nature. Although there are many forces that can keep this flower from blooming, it will always be a part of who we are. Thus when we return to it, it eventually feels right. As if this is how we were meant to be.

As we try new behaviors we tend to face some fear. Often this is the fear of failure. Until our confidence builds, we feel a little shaky. It's that heightened awareness of "Maybe I'm doing this wrong" which is a close cousin to "I might look foolish." Frequently the obstacle that stands between us and the development of new, healthy behaviors is *anxiety about making mistakes.*

Mistakes

Affirmation is an expression of appreciation for someone's special gifts. It is also an opinion. It's your belief that someone has a certain remarkable quality. Like every opinion, it could be wrong.

Sometimes you feel *sure* you see a real talent in someone. Other times, however, you're not so sure. You see some signs or what may be the beginnings of a special skill. But it could be wishful thinking. It may not seem right to encourage someone to pursue an endeavor when you're not convinced they have what it takes. You wouldn't want to set someone up for a failure. So maybe it's best to say nothing.

But it is precisely at these points that encouragement is needed most, when newborn talents are fragile, new, and perhaps unrecognized. Many abilities die before they are fully born. Their survival depends on whether someone perceptive and caring enough is there to nurture them. Someone willing to cheer for these qualities to live on.

We must be willing to affirm even without the luxury of knowing for sure that we are right. There can be sincerity without certainty. A music teacher who sees what may be early indications of a musical gift might say, "You may have talent here. I'm excited to see how you have progressed." This is not a promise, but rather an expression of possibility.

Telling someone, "You might be good at this," does not promise them success or set them up for disappointment. Instead, it nudges them to take a more thorough look at what might be a strength. It is an encouragement to consider taking another step in the development of this quality or skill. Good affirmation sometimes has a tentative tone to it. You don't have to be all-knowing or completely certain before expressing your belief that someone may have a special gift.

Even if you wind up being wrong, your kind words will still likely be valuable. Affirmation establishes a connection between people and this connection is always beneficial. Beyond this, every act of affirmation increases the likelihood that there will be *more* affirmation. You can be mistaken and still be a wonderful role model.

In order to be effective, however, *affirmation must be sincere.* Even those who are the best at it will sometimes make mistakes. No child has all the gifts her grandmother sees in her. Still, she is a better person for every kind word she's heard spoken to her.

Self-Affirmation

In recent years, more and more has been written about self-affirmation. It has become a well-known concept and has been endorsed by many as a necessary ingredient for good mental health.

Self-affirmation is typically described as the process of giving yourself encouraging statements such as "you're smart enough to do this," or "people will like you," or simply, "you can do it." Often the statements are repeated over and over again in an effort to give them power and credibility.

The growing interest in self-affirmation is itself interesting. But it is, at best, a partial solution to a much larger problem. We all need to be affirmed. We need to know that we are valued by others. *If, however, this need is not met, we will look for alternative solutions.* Enter *self*-affirmation.

In the long run, self-affirmation will never completely fill our need to be affirmed. It simply does not have enough power. In the short run, though, it can be helpful. Positive self-talk can steel our determination to face the audience or apply for the promotion. It can help us get back on our feet after a setback. Self-affirmation can give us a boost of confidence when we need it most. It's that little push that can get us over the hump.

Self-affirmation, however, will never replace real affirmation from others. Its effects are only temporary. I've never heard anyone say, "I remember that wonderful affirmation I gave myself ten years ago—it meant so much to me." Self-affirmation doesn't have the power to take root in our hearts like real affirmation does.

Self-affirmation becomes most helpful when it is supported by memories of *real* affirmation. It's easier to believe *you* can do it if *others* have told you that you can. Holding on to memories of encouraging words makes your own words of encouragement more effective. Memories of good affirmation are tremendously helpful in our pursuit of health and happiness.

There is a place, however, for positive self-talk. It can even help us begin to become more affirming. There may be occasions when it would help to say to ourselves something like, "He really has a gift for listening, and I'm going to tell him so," or "She really has been a good friend. It's time I let her know how much I appreciate her." This type of positive self-talk can help initiate new behaviors and sustain them as they gain strength.

As one grows in this art, affirmation becomes a lifestyle. One becomes more aware and more appreciative of the blessings we've been given. We should try to recognize and be grateful for these gifts. We must also remain diligent in our efforts to see the good in others and help them recognize the good in themselves.

CHAPTER FOUR
How to Affirm

*E*ffective affirmation tends to have certain ingredients, certain qualities that come together to create a powerful message. These qualities can be learned and, with practice, may become part of your lifestyle.

Having said this, I must make it clear that those who affirm well do so in their own way. There is an "X-factor," if you will, that is a personal quality that makes everyone's expression of affirmation unique. No two people who affirm well do so in exactly the same way. The art of affirmation is not a process you memorize and repeat. It is an art that requires a desire to help people grow, a particular set of skills, and the willingness to express your individuality.

This personal quality is essential because it communicates sincerity. Rote repetition does not convey honesty. The best affirmation is spoken in one's own language. Affirming well requires that you develop your personal style. It must be a sincere expression of you.

Some skilled affirmers are effusive and eloquent. Others use only a few words. Some use a lot of touch, others not so much. There are those who have mastered the art who prefer to use the written word. They express themselves well in letters, short notes, and e-mails. Then there are those who best practice the art in person. Others use a combination of many styles.

All those who affirm well, however, have something in common: *they make their affirmation believable*. They communicate sincerity. Even when individuals are not ready to accept that they have a particular gift, good affirmation leads them to consider the *possibility* that they have something special to offer. Accepting this possibility is a valuable beginning. Helping people get to the point where they realize "maybe I *can* do this" is quite a contribution. Good affirmers recognize the moments when their message is most likely to be received and then deliver that message effectively. In time, one's style of affirming may change.

This leads us to a fundamental lesson needed in learning how to affirm in your own unique way. You must learn from your experience. Every effort you make to affirm will provide you with new knowledge. Try to understand the information given you. Did the person hear you? Did he or she understand what you were saying? Could you have communicated it more effectively? Should you have said more? Less? Did you recognize how it impacted them? How did it affect bystanders who may have seen or heard you?

Like all art forms, learning to affirm can be a life-long process.

The Mind and the Heart

Good affirmation begins inside you. It takes shape before anyone but you knows it's there. It is a product of the mind and heart working together to do what you believe and feel to be right.

Good affirmation begins with an understanding of the importance of affirmation. This may be a gradual or sudden awakening. Affirmation is more than a nicety, it is a necessity. It does more than just help people feel good about themselves; it brings out the best in them. It helps them become everything they were meant to be.

This understanding creates a mindset; a mindset about how to make the world a better place; a mindset about how to improve the lives of those we touch. Through affirmation we have the ability to improve the world, one person at a time. The art of affirmation provides the tools to make this most significant contribution.

This mindset provides the map of how to help others grow toward their potential. It is a strategy to help people develop their gifts.

This knowledge will be of little consequence, however, without the *desire* to help people. It's not enough to know how to contribute; you have to *want* it. You have to want to use this art to produce great things. The best affirmers have a passionate desire to help others recognize and develop their blessings. The mind understands the need and develops the skills, but the heart feels the love, passion, and desire. Those most skilled in the art of affirmation are typically described as "good-hearted people." Actually, they use both their minds *and* their hearts.

Developing an Eye for Gifts

This particular facet of learning the art of affirmation may be the most enjoyable. There's no pain, no risk, and you get to see really beautiful things. As you get better at it, in fact, you see more and more beauty, because that is what this stage is all about: finding beauty.

It starts with a decision to look for the best in people. The process begins once this decision is made. Pick someone, anyone. Make a conscious effort to recognize his strengths. Look at his talents and virtues. Try to notice his attitudes. Listen to what others say about him. Are other people recognizing abilities that you've missed? Watch this person over time and, if possible, in a variety of contexts.

Look at people with an *eager eye*. Push yourself a little. Look with the mentality of a treasure-hunter. You know there's gold in there *somewhere*, you just have to find it. An eager eye searches with anticipation of finding something marvelous. The search is life-giving. It can be especially rewarding to find wonderful qualities in someone that no one had yet discovered.

The eager eye is motivated by the *desire* to see the best in people as well as the desire to see them grow to their potential. It is also fueled by a confidence in your abilities to see the best in people. With practice, this will improve. I've had people ask if this skill is learned or if some are born good at it. This is a tough question to answer. It certainly *seems* as though some people are natural-born treasure-hunters. These folks appear to have an innate gift for finding people's strengths. Their gift begins to appear at an early age and never really leaves them.

Having said this, I am equally certain that *everyone* can—and should—learn to recognize the gifts and virtues in others. We can, with practice, all improve our ability to find people's blessings.

Besides an eager eye, we must have a *patient* eye. We must be willing to wait for gifts to surface. Not every child's blessings will be apparent the first month of school. Many gifts take time to blossom. Looking through patient eyes, we accept that. Although someone does not seem to have a particular gift now, he or she may in time.

This is particularly important for those working with children. Psychological research has repeatedly demonstrated that teacher expectations strongly influence student performance. What this means, in a nutshell, is that when a teacher decides—however incorrectly—that a student does not have academic ability, that student is not likely to perform well with that particular teacher. When a teacher concludes that the ability is not there, it becomes less likely that the student's real abilities will surface.

Looking through patient eyes keeps us from making judgments too quickly. It acknowledges the possibility that someone's best qualities may not have shown themselves yet. One who continues growing will be continually revealing new features. In this process new strengths emerge. A blessing that isn't apparent today may become obvious in time. The art of affirmation requires that you be willing to wait, and hope, for the new gifts that have yet to be born.

The eager eye and the patient eye can easily coexist. This is demonstrated by parents who communicate to their children, "I love who you are and I'm excited about all that you will become." The mistake, of course, is to conclude that what you *see* is all there is. Then there would be no reason to continue looking for strengths. A blessing that is not visible today, however, may become recognizable tomorrow.

Practice looking for qualities in people. Look at the woman behind the counter in the crowded cafeteria. Is there anything to admire about her? What specifically? Look carefully at those around you. Can you detect any special qualities?

Because affirmation must be sincere, you must be honest about what you see. Anyone can make shallow observations such as "I'm sure she's a wonderful person."

Look closer! That woman behind the counter working in the heat and dealing with a line of customers who are in a hurry, what do you see in her that's special? BE SPECIFIC!

In the process of developing an eye for people's gifts, some find it easier to start with people close to them. Often it's easier to see the remarkable traits in loved ones and close friends. Look a little harder than you typically do. What do you observe? What do they have that makes them special? Think about it. Are there qualities you may have missed?

Whether you begin with strangers, loved ones, or both, the challenge here is to look a little harder, a little more deliberately. Look with enthusiasm—and with patience.

Methods of Affirmation

There are many ways to affirm. While everyone has his or her particular style, the most effective affirmers are comfortable with a variety of strategies. There is no one form of affirmation that reaches everyone. Some people are moved by public displays of affirmation. Others don't receive this as well. Some are more likely to accept affirmation if it is accompanied by touch. Others aren't comfortable with this physical gesture.

Many people are moved by *written* affirmation. They like to read and reread the message in privacy. Others feel more power from affirmation they receive in front of friends, family, or coworkers. Some people can only hear loud applause. Others prefer a quiet pat on the back.

The art of affirmation is not about selecting a favorite method for giving affirmation. It's not that simple! The art of affirmation is about continually learning new ways to affirm people and then matching the appropriate method with each individual. This involves developing a set of skills. It also means learning which methods are most effective with each individual.

Small expressions of encouragement are less likely to upset those who feel threatened by affirmation. A simple "thank you" or "good job" can sometimes sneak through even the most guarded person's defenses. A smile can be affirming. Taking the time to listen to someone can also be affirming. It communicates that you believe that she or he is worth listening to.

Using someone's name can be a form of affirmation. Calling a person by name says that the person is important to you, important enough to have remembered her name. Using her name also reminds her that you are focused on her. That you feel she is worthy of your time and attention. Addressing someone by name also helps establish the connection that is part of effective affirmation.

Affirmation can come through a variety of channels. It can be expressed through the spoken word, touch, or gestures. You can affirm someone by phone, voice mail, e-mail, text-messaging, and all the other emerging technologies that allow us to send our thoughts and feelings. You can affirm someone through notes, letters, or even singing telegrams. You can praise someone in private or in front of an audience—or both.

The most important question is *not* which form of affirmation do *I* like best. The most important question is, "How can I affirm this person in a way that will touch him or her?"

Some people might suggest that the best form of affirmation is the face-to-face approach. This would seem to be the most personal and, in most cases, it probably is. But sometimes the most important ingredients for good affirmation are sincerity and *permanence*. For example, I recently called a colleague after reading an article he had published. He wasn't in, so I left a heartfelt voice mail telling him how much I liked his writing. A day or so later he came to my office to tell me how much he appreciated my message. He said, *"I've listened to it four times already."*

Permanent affirmation (i.e., the written or recorded kind), though often delivered from a distance, has a special power since a person can keep these forever. It can be read and reread, or listened to again and again. It's my own theory that affirmation notes get read, on the average, at least ten times. (And the actual number may be higher than that.) People can take them to places where they feel most comfortable and let themselves absorb the words. This is not always possible with the spoken word, delivered in a social setting.

People who have trouble receiving affirmation may have an easier time accepting your words if they can do so in a place of their own choosing. If so, begin by sending them a message they can read or listen to in their comfort zones.

The art of affirmation is about developing a variety of methods to express encouragement. Another form of affirmation is the immediate, spontaneous, usually in person, variety. This type of affirmation may be less censored by the brain and thus more true to the heart. It's the "Wow!" "Way to go!" or "You are *so* good!" What it lacks in eloquence it makes up for in innocence and sincerity. It is childlike in its enthusiasm. Spontaneous affirmation brings vitality to relationships. It brings happiness to those who give it as well as those who receive it.

There are greeting cards that may help you express your admiration for someone. You can use someone else's words to help you get started. You can experiment with different styles of affirmation. Try to recall the most affirming people you've known. What did they do? What made them so effective? To learn the art of affirmation, you have to pay attention to the best affirmers in your own life.

Learn from experience and then be creative. Opportunities for affirmation can be easily missed. When I was in college, I felt affirmed by everyone who wanted to sign the cast on my broken hand. While growing up, I also felt affirmed when other kids asked me to sign *their* casts. The language of affirmation is a creative one. It is spoken most fluently by people who allow themselves to be creative.

I can affirm you with a hug, a note, a voice mail, or by asking you to sign my cast. While good affirmation often recognizes a specific strength ("I love your honesty"), it may also point to one's overall goodness ("I'm lucky to have you in my life"). Remember, for affirmation to be effective, it must reach its target and it must be delivered in the right way at the right time.

Timing

There are moments when people are more open to being affirmed. There are also times when they are not as willing to hear or believe anything positive you might have to say about them. While you might think that we should be eager to hear affirmation when we need it most, it doesn't always work that way. In fact, when we need it most we may be quite unwilling to believe it!

Discouraged individuals often have a difficult time accepting encouragement. They are reluctant to hear it. They *need* it, but they can't seem to *accept* it. It appears to bounce off them. Unless, of course, it is sent in a way, and at a moment, that allows it to penetrate their defenses.

Call these "reachable moments," times when someone is ready to receive affirmation. Part of the art of affirmation involves learning to recognize these openings. Certain moments are better than others. In these moments, kind words are more likely to be heard. In a reachable moment, affirmation is accepted and allowed to take root. These moments may be fleeting and easily missed, so we need to keep an eye out for these opportunities.

A good deal of affirmation is delivered in loud circumstances. There's the cheering that comes for an athlete at a sporting event, or the applause for a graduate as she walks across the stage for her diploma. Applauding for a child after his piano recital is also an affirming moment. Loud affirmation can be good for the soul. Cheering for someone is life-giving: it provides energy and confidence to those who send it and those who receive it. In these moments we are reminded how invigorating affirmation can be.

This type of affirmation is indeed powerful. Being appreciated by a group can produce healthy memories that may last forever. This kind of affirmation is a celebration of one's gifts. It is a ritual where a community expresses its appreciation of someone's character or abilities. Feeling appreciated in this way can have a very special impact.

Although we often think of affirmation as the voice of an audience, the opportunities for effective affirmation are even more likely to occur in quiet moments. A coworker sits slumped at his desk after hearing he did not get the promotion. A ten-year-old walks slowly behind his classmates after a particularly difficult day. Or a friend calls you for "no reason" and you just sense that she could use an encouraging word or two. In the art of affirmation there are times when you simply *feel* the opportunity. These moments are often quiet moments—and we must seize them!

In quiet moments there may be fewer distractions. It may be easier to hear what otherwise might be missed. In the more silent moments, there may also be greater opportunity for people to feel connected with each other. When you join someone in his or her solitude, you may find a very reachable moment.

The art of affirmation involves recognizing these moments when they present themselves and being prepared to act spontaneously. But this art can also involve planning. Sometimes you have to *arrange* the occasion for someone to become reachable. Sending a note, letter, or recording that reaches that person in an appropriate time and place can have lasting effects. Giving someone a message that she can hold on to until she reaches a place where she can soak it in is quite a gift. A gift that keeps giving.

Affirmation sometimes requires forethought. You have to ask yourself: What do I want to convey to this person? What is the most effective way to send this message? When might she or he be most open to receiving it?

The Attitude of Affirmation

Affirmation is ultimately an act of love. The art of affirmation is an art practiced by those willing to love. They love *people*. They love *life*. They love seeing people become all they are meant to be. Those who practice this art love to see others recognized for the good they have done. Ultimately, the greatest reward of affirmation is that it *spreads love*.

Affirmation is also *energy*. It fuels people to reach a little farther, climb a little higher. It encourages people to try a little harder and feel a bit more grateful.

Affirmation keeps the human spirit moving in the right direction.

Affirmation is a *loving* act. It is also frequently an assertive behavior. It requires *courage*. This is especially true in contexts (and there are many of them) that have not encouraged affirmation. Most of us have experienced families, classrooms, or workplaces that have all but posted signs that say: WORDS OF ENCOURAGE-MENT NOT SPOKEN HERE.

The brave souls who challenge these unhealthy rules must be assertive, determined, and, sometimes, a little thick-skinned. We will all encounter people and places that do not value, or understand, the power of affirmation. In order to develop in this art, you must be prepared to practice it in places that have not supported it or seen it done well. You have to be willing to bring it to places where it has never been.

Those who affirm well not only change people, they change *places*. An affirming boss can change the atmosphere of an entire company. An encouraging principal can lift the spirits of a school.

I sometimes refer to assertiveness as the secret ingredient in the art of affirmation. There are people who have the skills and sensitivity to be good at it, but their talent seldom sees the light of day. They may have the desire but not the moxie. Affirmation involves acting on the conviction that expressing recognition and apprecia-tion for someone's blessings is the right thing to do. It means daring to affirm, even in contexts that have not encouraged or supported affirmation. The act of affirmation is a sign of *strength*. It is practiced most effectively by those with the courage to make their voices heard.

Assertiveness adds strength to affirmation. This strength makes the message more believable. This is true even when you are only pointing to someone's potential. You may tell a person something like "you may well have a gift for writing." Although this merely suggests the *possibility* that a gift exists, it can be stated in a confident way. In other words, an affirmation can be both tentative *and* strong.

If you believe the affirmation you are sending, and if you can communicate your conviction, it is more likely that the person you are affirming will believe it as well.

Assertiveness is an especially important quality for those who have not been as affirming as they would like to be. New behaviors can be frightening. Jumping off the diving board for the first time takes real courage. This is especially true for those who have not had good role models. It's hard to start something when you're just not sure you can do it.

I love the advice given by therapist and author Melody Beattie on how to begin healthy new behaviors. She writes, "Start where you are. Start poorly. Just begin. Let yourself fumble, be awkward and confused. If you already knew how to do it, it wouldn't be a lesson in your life. And you wouldn't get the thrill of victory two, five or ten years from now when you look back and say, 'Wow. I've gotten good at that over time.'"[1]

Effort is more important than outcome, especially in the beginning. Even when your efforts fall on deaf ears, *keep trying*. Remember, a key to learning this art, or any art, is to learn from experience. Turn failures into lessons and lessons into successes. Find the methods you are most comfortable with and start there. Work on your timing. Study how others affirm and learn from them. But allow yourself to have your own personal style.

Your technique can be flawed. Your timing can be off. You can stumble and bumble your way to a powerful affirmation. But you must be sincere. You must courageously speak what is in your heart. Stay away from flattery. Flattery is like fool's gold. Sooner or later people realize they've been deceived. Then they may doubt even the most genuine affirmation.

Don't complicate this simple art. Keep it simple. Learn from each experience, and above all, keep it sincere.

CHAPTER FIVE
Through the Years

*A*ffirmation means supporting the best in people. The hunger for this support continues throughout life. People of all ages need to know they are appreciated. This need, however, changes over time. Each stage of life has its special strengths and uncertainties. To affirm well, you must recognize the needs and the language of each stage. This is not a one-size-fits-all process. Each phase of life presents certain challenges and opportunities. In the art of affirmation, you must consider the developmental needs of the person whom you wish to affirm.

Children

Children must believe they are valued in order to grow up valuing themselves. They need to know that they are loved. They need to hear that they have something valuable to offer. It's a simple formula: children internalize the praise and encouragement they receive. That is, they record it and take it with them through life. If children receive enough affirmation, delivered in an effective manner, they build a solid foundation on which to construct confidence and character.

The *sense* of being valued comes through the *experience* of being valued. Every encounter with sincere affirmation creates such an experience. Children need to know that who they are and the qualities they possess are recognized and appreciated by others. It's through this appreciation that they come to value themselves.

Children need to know they are lovable just as they are. Just as important, they need occasional assurances that they have emerging powers that will allow them to grow into even more wonderful beings. They need to know that they are valued for who they are and who they are becoming.

By affirming children, you teach them that there are encouraging people in the world. This makes the planet safer and much more welcoming. At the same time, you are helping them learn to recognize affirming people. This is an essential skill. If you want children to receive adequate encouragement throughout their lives, help them to learn to recognize and appreciate affirming people.

Help children to listen to words of encouragement. Teach them how to accept these messages graciously. Help them become people who are easy to affirm, who accept praise with a polite "thank you" rather than an argument about how they are really not that good. Let them know it's not rude, shallow, or vain to accept encouragement. Help them learn that the appropriate response is usually a simple but sincere expression of gratitude. Children who know how to *accept* affirmation are more likely to *receive* it.

When offering encouragement to children, be as specific as possible. Children are concrete thinkers. Most don't yet have the ability to abstract. Avoid statements such as, "You have a wonderful sense of beauty," or "You have a remarkable appreciation of justice." Instead, try something like, "You really are a good painter," or "I like the way you try to be fair with your friends."

Point to individual skills and then always look for themes. A boy who is good at soccer and swimming should be reminded from time to time that he is a gifted athlete. Support your words with specific examples of his abilities. Another child who is a class leader, a marvelous babysitter, and a good friend should be reassured that she is developing wonderful people skills. Again, point to concrete examples of her strengths. As they age, their recognition of these themes will become more and more important. No single gift will carry them through life. Children must begin to discover the range of their blessings and understand how to integrate their collection of gifts.

Understanding their strengths (as well as their limitations) is essential to the process of building an identity. We want children to believe they are valued and that they have their own set of skills and talents. We want them to enjoy developing new virtues and abilities. We want them to see the world as an affirming place where people will value them for who they are and what they have to offer—a place where people are rooting for them to become everything they can be. We would like them to be surrounded by role models who affirm well.

In a perfect world they would always be among people who support and cheer for them. But we know this may not be the case. We can't assume that they will always be offered the encouragement they need. Thus it is all the more important that they collect good affirming memories in childhood, memories that will last should they travel through unaffirming contexts.

Getting your affirmation to stick with someone is an essential goal in the art of affirmation. Creativity and timing are both important. Unique or unusual expressions of affirmation tend to be memorable. The often-told story of the grade school teacher who had her fourth grade students write the best qualities of all their classmates makes this point. She collected the affirmations and gave each student a list of all the good things classmates said about her or him. Then, many years later, at the funeral of one of the students, the teacher discovered that most of the students still had their lists. In fact, some of them carried them in their wallets and purses.

These kids probably did not have another teacher take the same approach. It was unique. The affirmations they gave each other were concrete, tangible (i.e., on paper), and given in a creative way. These lists were carried and recalled when needed. These are all the ingredients to remember when affirming children.

Besides being *creative*, you may also have to be *persistent*. Some children resist praise. Some don't know how to respond to it. Others have trouble believing it. In an effort to avoid it, they distract themselves. It's as if they turn off their hearing. You may get a slight smile or a little nod but it's not at all clear they heard what you said. With enough practice at this, they can wall themselves off from all discouragement.

After affirming such a child, it may be appropriate to ask her, "Did you hear what I said?" This should not be asked in a scolding tone but, rather, in a warm, supportive voice. You may even need to follow this by requesting that she tell you what she heard. If she did not get the full message, repeat it to her. Sending an affirming message isn't enough. You have to do what you can to make sure it is received.

Children should also receive "official" affirmation. This is the kind of affirmation that is signed, stamped, and somehow made permanent. It's the Scout badge, the certificate, or the trophy—the kind of thing they can hang on their wall and stare at in good times and bad. I've long thought that every report card should include a clear affirming statement. No matter how poorly a student does, a teacher should be required to write on the report some mention of that child's strengths. If a teacher cannot find a single strength, that student should not be in that classroom.

Clearly there are times when children need to be corrected and disciplined. I am not suggesting that recognizing their gifts will replace the need to control and, occasionally, punish them. But in an environment where they feel appreciated, and where they believe they are capable of making worthy contributions, there will be less need for punishment.

Children would rather be good than bad. One of the most effective ways to help children *be* good is to convince them that they *are* good. Every adult who lives and works with children shares the responsibility of helping them find their goodness.

Look for the gifts that might be missed. While everyone may appreciate a child's athletic abilities, they may miss his efforts to be kind to people. Look for the beginnings of virtues and abilities. Affirm the gifts that are not being affirmed. Praise a noble effort even if the results are not what one hoped for. Put energy into the fragile beginnings of blessings.

When children are adequately affirmed, they learn *how* to affirm. They collect role models, people who affirmed them in their own unique way. They will accumulate memories of being affirmed—with all the love and protection this brings—and they will gather skills and techniques of affirmation. Every affirming character in their lives becomes a teacher of the art of affirmation. I repeat, when children are affirmed well, they learn how to affirm.

Adolescence

Within this relatively brief period of time young people go through significant changes. The young adolescent (i.e., age thirteen) is, in many ways, quite different from the nineteen-year-old. Many thirteen-year-olds, for example, are still concrete thinkers. As with younger children, use specific examples when pointing to their good qualities. To a nineteen-year-old it would be appropriate to say, "You have *real* musical abilities." To a younger adolescent, however, you are usually better off to begin by suggesting, "You played that piece really well." If you are unsure which approach will be most effective (for instance, with a sixteen-year-old or a more mature thirteen-year-old), use both. Move from the specific to the general or more abstract: "You did a great job organizing the food drive. It appears you have some strong leadership abilities."

Most simple skills point to larger abilities. A boy who can clean fish well may have good hand-eye coordination. A girl who is in demand as a babysitter may be mature and responsible, or have a gift for understanding and working with people. Look for the patterns and the themes. They may be pointing the adolescent toward a particular calling.

Keep in mind that the adolescent world is not always an affirming place. This is particularly true during early adolescence. At this age, kids are so concerned about fitting in with their social circle that they spend little time or energy encouraging each other. Their focus is on themselves. While it may seem that they spend every hour of every day with their friends, it can be a lonely time of life. The interpersonal connections do not yet run as deep as they may seem.

Self-esteem often reaches a low point around age thirteen.[1] While this is a time when they truly need positive feedback, young adolescents are not always receptive to it. They frequently present a façade that seems to say, "Leave me alone," or "I don't need your nice little words." This, of course, is anything but true. Affirming young adolescents is a special challenge because even though they need it, they may not give an appreciative response when you try to encourage them. When you affirm adolescents, especially younger ones, you have to believe in what you're doing. You have to believe in it enough to continue with it, even when you don't hear anything remotely resembling a thank you.

Teenagers need affirmation and, in spite of the façade, will accept it and take it to heart. But perhaps more than any other time in life, adolescents are particular about whom they will allow to affirm them. It may be the football coach, guitar teacher, or their friend's really cool parent. It could be the teacher they couldn't manipulate or the one who seems most willing to listen. Often it is someone they decide is most *real*. To adolescents this sense of *real* means someone who is believable, someone who is not affirming them because she wants them to behave better or study harder. Someone who is not even *trying* to get them to like her, and the only reason she is telling them something good about themselves is that she sees it and recognizes its value.

In your efforts to affirm adolescents, this will be the test you will need to pass. You must be perceived as real. Look inside yourself. Try to understand your motives. Psychiatrist Conrad Baars once wrote, "Affirmation is a gift freely given with no strings attached."[2]

Teenagers are always looking for the strings. To affirm teenagers well, you must know your own agenda. Wait until you can give the gift freely before trying to affirm.

While affirming adolescents, you must pay close attention to the audience. Some encouragement is best done directly. This is especially true when you recognize what may be an unwelcome talent emerging. A young man may not want you to praise his poetry in front of the class. Until he becomes more confident, this affirmation may be better given in private. Similarly, you may see the beginnings of a rich spirituality in a teenager but opt to point to this gift in a one-on-one situation. Some special qualities are more likely to surface in front of small audiences.

Adolescents are particularly sensitive to how they are perceived by others. They can, and often do, hide their gifts for fear that these gifts may alienate them from their peer group. A colleague of mine once told me how he used to hide his musical side. He was raised in a tough neighborhood and he didn't want his friends to know that he loved to play the saxophone. In order to balance his desire to play in the school band with his fear of disappointing his friends, he would awaken in the wee hours and walk to school with his saxophone before his friends were up to see him. A lot of teenagers find themselves in this situation. They have gifts that they are not ready for the world to see. Sometimes they need to be affirmed privately.

Early in adolescence teens focus a lot of attention on themselves. As time passes this should change. More and more they notice the needs and the strengths of those around them. As these qualities develop, they may begin to be more affirming. If these skills are reinforced, they will grow. This is a tremendously important development. Adolescent environments—such as high school, youth groups, teams, or clubs— function best when the members affirm each other. Teens see gifts that others miss. The encouragement they offer to each other may be more credible than when it comes from some adults. Good adolescent role models help produce the healthiest adolescent environments.

In all cases, when you affirm an adolescent, do so respectfully. Teenagers are not likely to feel affirmed if you address them as you would a young child. They are sensitive to this. Addressing them respectfully is itself an affirmation.

When I was a freshman in college, I had a writing teacher who possessed a rather basic yet wonderfully effective style of affirmation. She seemed to have few reservations about calling us on our mistakes. At first we protected ourselves by agreeing she was incompetent. Yet, in time, it became clear she knew what she was doing. She was direct yet always respectful. She could reduce your masterpiece to a sea of red ink. Still, she seemed to know the pain of a wounded artist.

The young professor taught three sections of freshman English. Every other Thursday we all handed in essays. All sixty, or so, students had them back the following Tuesday.

I had never been a great student. But I liked this class. For a long time I had a fantasy about becoming a writer. I never told anyone, though, as I thought it was only a pipe dream. This class, however, stirred something in me. I began to think "maybe."

When the semester ended, I received one of the few As in any of her classes. I had never cared a great deal about grades but this one felt glorious. The dream was still alive. At eighteen I thought this was by far the most important affirmation I had received in school. Then something even more important came a few months later.

After that first semester, I immersed myself in writing. I thought outside the box and colored outside the lines. I searched for my own style of writing. I experimented. And I was reminded that experiments sometimes fail. The semester was filled with good grades and not so good ones.

Throughout the course, this professor met regularly with each of her students. As the semester entered its final days, we met for the last time. We reviewed my most recent essay. Then her face took on both a smile and a frown as if to say, "I have some good news and some bad news."

"You know you're not going to receive the same grade you did last semester," she began. This wasn't a surprise. Those failed experiments may make one a better writer but they don't help the grade. "But," she slowly added as the smile chased the frown, "when I get home on Thursday nights with my pile of papers, I always read yours first."

A year earlier I would not have understood the importance of this. I might not even have realized it was much of a compliment. As a student, and a concrete thinker, the goal is the grade. But now, at eighteen, I wanted more than this. I wanted to be a writer. I wanted to have an impact. The grade didn't mean as much anymore. Being *read first*, however, meant everything.

This writing instructor knew how to affirm a young writer because she knew what it was to like to be a young writer. She could reach an eighteen-year-old because she remembered what it was like to be eighteen. She understood the hopes and insecurities, the secret and fragile dreams.

Good affirmation requires respect and empathy. These qualities are especially important in your efforts to affirm adolescents.

Young Adulthood

Adolescents need to know they can make it in the group. Young adults need to know they can make it on their own. The twenties and early thirties are about becoming established. During this time a person wants to know that he can survive, find a meaningful vocation, and build healthy relationships. This age group also wants to feel appreciated. They need to know that they matter, that what they have and what they do are valued. They may doubt, however, that genuine affirmation actually exists in the *real world*.

Much of young adulthood can be described as a search for affirmation. Because so many of us mistakenly believe that the need for affirmation only exists in *children*, there is a shortage of this treasure in the *adult* world. The competition for the available supply can be fierce. It can be tempting to conclude that affirmation doesn't even live in the land of grown-ups.

If people cannot find affirmation, they will look for a replacement. Some will try to collect money as a sign that they are good at something. Others will look to accumulate power as proof of their worth. Neither of these, though, can meet the need to be reassured by another human being. Money and power will always feel empty without sincere affirmation.

Entering young adulthood is like finally stepping out on stage. There have been years of preparation and rehearsal for this grand entrance into adulthood. Every teacher you ever had told you this was coming. This is the "when you grow up" that they were always talking about. All the roads of your past have led to this arrival. Now the young adult is forced to face the question: "Am I prepared to survive in the adult world?"

This is fertile ground for self-doubts. They are doubts that are usually carried in secret. No one wears a sign that says: "I'm scared and I need someone to tell me I know what I'm doing!" Although the sign is not there, the feelings often are. Young adulthood is a time of quiet yet intense need for affirmation. The need is strong yet, typically, unspoken.

One solution is *mentoring*. Young adults, often eager to free themselves from authority figures, may overlook this opportunity. This is a stage where they may enjoy more freedom than ever. Guidance may feel like restriction or, even, manipulation. Thus they may avoid those who might effectively nurture and coach them. In so doing, they may distance themselves from would-be mentors who could help them recognize and achieve their potential.

As an example, consider *the first boss*. Standing at the gate to the adult world is this soul. The young adult may have had jobs as a teenager, but this is different. That was about making a little money; this is about survival. The first real boss has the power to indicate whether or not you can make it in the adult world. Her opinion of your abilities matters. If she sees you as lacking talent, you have no experience to contradict her, no strong list of successes. But if she sees abilities, or even just potential, suddenly you have a future.

Career paths are plotted here. At this age, a person wants to know, "Do I have a future?" "Can I survive in the *real* world?" When one feels confident in her gifts, she will plan a bold, daring, ambitious future. Without this confidence, she will—as they say—*settle*. She will settle for less than what she could be. She is less likely to reach for the stars.

The first boss is important because this is someone who can help a young person recognize his or her potential. An affirming boss helps keep the dream alive.

This can be a shaky time. Young adulthood is time for perfecting the façade of competence. You have to look like you know what you're doing, even when you've never done *it* before. Young parents struggle to convince their children that they really *are* capable mothers and fathers. In each job interview they must convince the powers-that-be (e.g., the potential first boss) that they are *the* perfect candidate. They have to do this without having the experience to support their apparent confidence. Young adults frequently feel they have to appear more competent than they really are.

The mask of confidence can disguise their need for reassurance. It can keep them from searching for, or staying in touch with, those who might recognize both their needs and abilities. This persona of self-assurance can prevent them from connecting with mentors who might recognize their doubts and provide the direction and affirmation needed to help them become the best they can be.

Young adults want to appear *able*. They want their friends, families, and employers to see them as competent. Deep inside, though, they are looking to convince themselves. They want to know they have what it takes to live well in the adult world. They need to be reassured. This is the bind of young adulthood: They desperately need affirmation. They *need* to know they have the qualities necessary to succeed. But in their efforts to present an image of competence and self-sufficiency, they mask this essential need. To admit this need might shatter the image they are trying to project.

Those who seek to affirm young adults must understand this bind. At this age, they may not appear to need affirmation. They may not even express much gratitude when encouragement is offered them. But things are not always as they seem. This need is real.

The art of affirmation involves recognizing the need even when it is not obvious. It involves realizing its importance even when there is little or no visible indication. You may be sincerely thanked years from now, but today it may appear that they barely heard what you said.

Say it anyway!

Middle Age

Middle age is a time of life that keeps getting pushed back. People at forty tend to think of middle age as beginning at forty-five. Those at forty-five seem to think it starts at fifty. As our life expectancy continues to increase, there are indeed valid reasons to make these adjustments.

For our purposes, though, I am describing middle age as that span between the late thirties and the late fifties. These are the years of the infamous "midlife crisis." It is also a time when many people experience a great deal of happiness and success.

This time of life includes one's peak earning years. The combination of energy, health, and experience can make this a time of great accomplishment. Personal power may be at its height. By now, people are more likely to have found their niches. Energy is more likely to have found a focus. This focus, in turn, can produce a feeling of being settled.

Every age has its blessings and middle age is certainly no exception. Many people in leadership roles are middle-aged. This stage can be so comfortable it's easy to fall into the "I've-found-my-place-and-I-never-need-to-change" mode of thinking.

The so-called midlife crisis is not so much about too much change in a person's life, far more often it's about *an unwillingness to change*. Marriages fail during these years because some men and women refuse to change and grow. The road may feel safe and predictable but the scenery can become repetitious. Feeling *settled* deteriorates into feeling *stuck*. People can get complacent and stop opening new doors—doors that would lead them to where they need to be.

Emotional well-being, at this point, involves building stability *and* developing new, emerging abilities. It's about recognizing old trophies yet creating new goals. It's about appreciating what one has while allowing for change. It's about moving forward while being tempted to retreat into cozy comfort zones.

As we age, our abilities and priorities change. The driven executive who once routinely worked fourteen-hour days may have to accept that his once unlimited supply of energy is now indeed limited. This loss, however, may be replaced with knowledge and wisdom. He may not work as hard—but now works *smarter*. His aggressiveness may be replaced by patience. His ability to push people to perform may be replaced with a desire to nurture them toward their potential. His skill for making and saving money may give way to a growing generosity.

Good affirmation helps people grow *at any stage of life*. It helps people grow into what they are meant to be. During midlife, affirmation is a reminder that there is room for growth. Often it is a reminder that this growth is not only possible, it is necessary.

Recently my friend Rick provided me with an example of this. Rick is in his early fifties and has a son and a daughter, both young adults. He told me, "The other day some lady asked me if I had any grandchildren. I couldn't believe it. Nobody ever asked me that before. I was kind of stunned."

He took a moment before finishing his story. In that moment he seemed to be thinking hard about something.

"When I told her 'no,' she told me that I would make a good grandfather."

After another half a moment of quiet he added, "I don't think I'm ready to be called *Grandpa*, but—as I thought about it—it was kind of nice to hear her say that."

Rick was still a little confused by the whole thing. A few years ago he may have been offended by the lady's question. Even now it unsettled him a bit. It was, however, a wonderful affirmation. Well timed. Well delivered. Simple and sincere. It helped him lift his eyes and look a little farther down the road. It helped him recognize a gift he had not considered, a gift that may be quite valuable to him.

Those who focus on what they've lost may feel despair. But those who can see and appreciate their developing gifts live with hope. They understand that life changes. They realize that new blessings emerge in time. The healthiest people, at any stage of life, know that new talents and positive traits continue to appear regardless of age. There are always more blessings on the way.

Midlife can be a wonderful time. It can also be a time when people resist the changes they need to make. Their image of health and happiness is also their image of youth. They may see the blessings of youth fade and not recognize or appreciate the gifts of aging as they emerge. It is essential that others help them see and understand the value of these gifts. If they are fortunate, they have people in their lives who will help them discover their hidden treasures. People who eagerly and patiently watch for positive qualities to begin to show themselves.

So many of us mistakenly believe that growth slows as we approach our middle years. This myth creates a mindset. If we stop believing in something, we stop looking for it. If we understand that midlife can be a time of significant growth, we prepare ourselves to see all the goodness waiting to surface.

Affirmation in midlife is about seeing the fragile new gifts that are tucked behind older, more established talents. It's about helping people recognize, appreciate, and actualize these gifts. This is a time when new, often surprising, blessings appear. The detective finds a skill for gardening. The accountant recognizes in himself a renewed love for people. The housewife finds she has a knack for fundraising for her church.

There are always more blessings. This time of life is no different from the earlier stages in that we are continuously developing into more than what we were.

The crisis of midlife is frequently rooted in a lack of affirmation. With the possible exception of childhood, affirmation is as important now as at any other time in life. Learning the art of affirmation involves recognizing those who need to hear that they have something valuable to offer. People in midlife may be the most overlooked group of people who are in need of affirmation.

After Midlife

I don't know that anyone has found the perfect way to describe this time of life. They've been called the "golden years," but this stage has also been referred to as "old age." Maybe they're both accurate. Perhaps these are the best times *and* the times of greatest challenge.

As people move toward and then into their retirement years, their store of experience grows rich and full. They've known endings and beginnings, losses and acquisitions. They've been educated, humbled, challenged, and blessed. All this has led them toward an opportunity to understand the human condition. It is in this stage that people are most likely to understand the need for and the power of affirmation.

If you are new to the practice of affirmation, you may want to begin developing your skills with this population. Older people tend to better understand the need. They listen more. They are less likely to disqualify, minimize, or ridicule your message. They respond not only with their words but with their eyes. One of the blessings of aging is the gift of gratitude. As we age, many of us learn to say thank you with our entire being.

As with all stages of development, this can be a time of continuous growth. While at some point a certain physical decline begins, there is tremendous potential for spiritual and emotional growth. Many people see their most important abilities come alive during these years. For a lot of us, it's what we do *after* retirement that matters most.

Because people at this stage have accumulated so many experiences, there is much to affirm. Each spoken memory presents an opportunity to find a strength. There is a chance to discover something remarkable that someone has done with his or her life. We all want to know that we have lived well. As we age, however, this need becomes increasingly powerful. One of the greatest pains of aging is to be without people who will recognize and appreciate our contributions.

As we age, we need to speak the story of our lives. Part of this need involves the hope of being affirmed. If a listener does not understand this need, the stories may appear to be without purpose.

Remember, the need for affirmation is often *unspoken*. People don't usually say things such as, "Please tell me I made good decisions." Instead, we tell our stories to each other and hope others understand what we need to hear. Beyond this, because many of us have lost touch with our need for affirmation, *we* don't always realize what we're looking for. When the need for affirmation is misunderstood, important conversations may appear confusing and, perhaps, pointless.

When anyone tells their stories, look for opportunities to affirm. Interest in their story is itself an affirmation. Telling our stories helps us make sense of our lives. It keeps our minds active. It is a natural inclination that attempts to meet several needs. Important among these needs is the need to hear that someone values who we've been and what we've done. We'd like to know that our lives have somehow meant something.

As important as it is, though, affirming the *past* is not enough. As with people in all other phases of life, older persons need to be affirmed for who they are now and for who they are becoming. A workaholic doctor, for example, retires and soon feels lost. He's done many wonderful things with his life but now he must find a new path. This man would benefit from someone pastoral enough to point to his as yet unrecognized abilities. Affirmation, at this time, carries the message: "You can make more contributions. You're not finished." This helps maintain meaning and purpose in someone's life.

After retirement, a person is no longer looking for raises or promotions. These are yesterday's affirmations. At this time of life, people want to be reassured they can still live their lives in meaningful ways. They can hide out in safe little shelters or they can continue to learn, explore, and contribute. Those who fly beyond their comfort zones are often those who are surrounded by a strong supporting cast. They have invited people into their lives who encourage them through the first shaky steps into new territory.

Many mature adults have mastered the art of affirmation. Over time they have developed a deep understanding of this art. At some level, they have come to realize that their affirmations will become their legacy. They will be remembered for how they contributed. They will live on through their kindnesses and words of encouragement.

Those who affirm well are remembered well. Every time we help someone recognize their worth, we achieve a kind of immortality. When we help someone grow, we become a part of them. A part that may well, in some way, be passed on to someone else.

Eighty-year-old author Lois Leiderman Davitz recently told me, "Affirmation is a must at any age." She then added, "Perhaps even more so with increasing years."

It must be given. It must be received.

CHAPTER SIX
Receiving Affirmation

*I*t was meant to be an honest expression of appreciation, but I ended up feeling embarrassed. I guess I made him uncomfortable.

I was in my second year of college. The first semester had ended and I stopped by a professor's office to tell him I had liked his class. I had sensed he didn't get much encouragement from his students. But I genuinely liked his course, and I decided to tell him so.

I had never done this before. I assumed it would be simple. You just knock on the door and tell the guy you enjoyed his class. He says thanks for coming by, and you leave feeling good.

Well, that's the way it *should* work. But often it doesn't. That's one of the reasons there is a shortage of affirmation.

At first everything went as planned. I knocked on his door and he stepped out into the hall. So far so good. Then the wheels fell off. I told him I had just dropped by to tell him how much I liked his class. But instead of "thanks for coming by," he seemed confused and unsure of what to say. It occurred to me that he might be suspecting that I had ulterior motives. That maybe I was there to get him to change my grade. He looked at me as if to say, "Why are you *really* here?"

After an awkward silence we parted. As I walked away, I told myself, "I'll never do *that* again!" And I didn't. Over the next two and a half years of college and the following four years of graduate school, I never went back to affirm a teacher again.

If I had to do it again, I would affirm most of them—even the ones who don't accept affirmation well. After all, they're often the ones who may need it most. But at nineteen, I was new to the art of affirmation and more fragile than I wanted to believe. A single, relatively small, uncomfortable experience led me to keep my feelings of appreciation and admiration to myself far too long.

Not only do many of us struggle to affirm, many of us have difficulty accepting affirmation. It feels embarrassing, or we just never learned how to receive it. Maybe we've convinced ourselves that we are without remarkable qualities. Or perhaps we are uncomfortable with the personal closeness that may develop when someone encourages us. Whatever the reason, when we refuse affirmation, we cripple our own growth. Furthermore, we may discourage those who would like to be more affirming.

In a sense, we need to affirm the affirmer. We should avoid the situation where someone who tried to affirm us walked away saying, "I'll never do *that* again!"

People with low self-esteem often do this without ever realizing it. They refuse to accept praise. A coworker will compliment a presentation they made and they respond with, "Are you kidding?" Or a friend says something nice about a cake they baked and they barely acknowledge the comment. These responses decrease the likelihood that they will continue receiving positive feedback. Then, without this affirmation, their self-esteem deteriorates further.

Among those starving for affirmation are people who have been given a good deal of it. They wall themselves off from reassurances and encouragement. Sometimes their defenses are so automatic that the message doesn't even register. They can become virtually deaf to positive feedback.

I've worked with many clients who have mastered the art of *avoiding* affirmation. At times, you can almost see the wall spring up as you try to affirm them. Often I have them write an affirmation list. On this list I have them record all the affirming messages they can remember receiving. It can be sad to watch what they produce. Sometimes it's just one or two fleeting memories with little detail and little, if any, emotion.

So we begin there. We examine each memory, trying to flesh it out. Like Dickens' Scrooge, with the Ghost of Christmas Past, they may do their best to turn away. If they can hold their focus, however, the spell breaks. The wall begins to crumble, and more and more memories move to the surface. Their lists get longer, fuller, richer. All the kindness and encouragement that went unnoticed is now before them. This new awakening can drastically alter their perception of themselves and their world. Suddenly they have their own cheering section. A cheering section that includes their grandparents, the crossing guard from first grade, the lady who kept coming back to their lemonade stand, and every good teacher, coach, and friend they've ever had.

It's important to hold on to the memories of affirming people. Affirmation is not meant to be disposable: it's a gift that is meant to be lasting.

Receiving affirmation is much like receiving any other valuable gift—it should be treated respectfully. It ought to be put in a special place where it is protected. It should be stored somewhere inside you that is well lit and accessible so that you can return to it. Then you need to let those who affirm you know how much it means to you.

The process of accepting affirmation can be broken down into five steps. Though this entire process can take place in a matter of seconds, it's important that attention be given to all five steps:

1. *Show respect for the person and the message.* Affirmation often takes courage. This is especially true for those

people who are new to it. Don't dismiss them with a shallow "Oh it was nothing!" If it was nothing to them, they wouldn't have said anything! Even if you suspect you are being flattered or manipulated, accept it gracefully. Flattery may be a person's first step toward real affirmation. Besides, you may find that what at first *seemed* insincere may be quite real.

In order to respect affirmation, you have to be open to it. This is difficult for a lot of people. They'll convince themselves that the message isn't sincere, all because they've shut themselves off from affirmation. You have to allow yourself to hear kind words.

2. *Listen.* Let yourself hear what is being said. Sit with it for a moment. Consider it. It won't turn you into an egomaniac. Interestingly enough, good affirmation tends to be humbling. Rather than arrogance, it more often leads to feelings of gratitude.

Try to avoid interrupting the person. Affirmation is good for both parties. If at all possible hear him out. We have a need to *be affirmed*, but we also have a need *to affirm.* Allow him to affirm. You will be doing him a service.

It's not enough to hear what is being said. *You must listen.* Pay attention to the words that are being spoken or the lines that have been written. Feel the feeling behind the words. Let yourself be moved. Let yourself be grateful for those willing to encourage you.

3. *Respond sincerely.* Remember, good affirmation creates an opportunity for a connection between people. Whether or not this connection develops depends, in

part, on how affirmation is received. Give yourself permission to feel grateful for the kind words. Show your gratitude. Don't hide behind a mask of nonchalance. *Be real.* You can fumble for the right words if necessary. You don't have to be smooth, just honest.

These first steps benefit both you and the person affirming you. You are communicating that you are open to affirmation. You are letting people know that it is safe to affirm you. By listening respectfully and responding sincerely you are letting others know that you are willing to be affirmed. You are telling them that they will not be ignored or dismissed, should they tell you what you mean to them. In doing so, you are encouraging them to be more affirming.

4. *Store the message carefully.* If it is a spoken affirmation, take a moment to register it in your memory. Underline it, highlight it, put it somewhere safe inside you. If you really let yourself hear the message and let yourself sit with it for a moment or two, it becomes more likely that you will be able to retrieve it when you need it.

Similarly, there are certain written affirmations you should keep. They could be thank you notes, graduation cards, professional letters of recommendation, or even messages written in crayon. *Good affirmation is timeless.* A time may come when it will be a blessing to read them again. These days may come years after the words were written. Store them carefully.

Another reason to hold on to good affirmation is that it will serve as an example of how to affirm well.

Keeping these examples near or within you can help you develop in the art of affirmation. Hold on to your role models, even long after they're gone.

5. *Learn from the experience.* What have you learned from the person who has affirmed you? Could she be right? Could you have this gift that she seems to recognize? How does it feel to be affirmed? Does it help to be around affirming people? Is their style of affirmation effective?

Each affirmation you receive should make you better at giving and receiving it. You should learn from the encouragement you receive as well as the encouragement you give. Always keep in mind that learning from experience is essential to learning the art of affirmation.

Keep in mind too that no matter how good you get at accepting affirmation, there are situations that call for a creative response. Sometimes things get tricky. For example, I sometimes get complimented on my sense of color. Specifically, I've had people tell me that they like the way my tie, shirt, and pants "go together." Well the fact is, I have absolutely *no* sense of color. What I do have is a *wife* who has a good sense of color!

If time permits, I explain where the talent lies, and tell the person I will relay her compliment to my wife. But there have been times, I admit, when time did not allow for an explanation. In these cases, I've simply said thank you. I've long believed that the most important outcome of such an exchange is that the person leave feeling good that he or she took the time to affirm me.

Not all the praise you receive will be correct. Still, you are fortunate to be in the presence of someone willing to affirm you, even if that person overestimated your talent.

I also run into this sometimes with my writing. I'll have people tell me how much they liked something they read in one of my books. I then realize that what they're saying isn't even in the book! I don't think I've ever corrected someone in this situation. I try to respect what he or she is saying, listen carefully, and then respond with something like, "Thank you for reading the book. I really appreciate your taking the time to share your thoughts." There's always a smile and almost always a handshake. Again, the person should leave feeling *good* about what he or she has done.

Concerning what people *thought* they read in the book, well, maybe they've confused it with another book—or perhaps they've made a unique interpretation of something I've written. (Which, by the way, is valuable information for a writer.) Or it could be they've recognized something quite obvious that I've missed in my own writing. In any case, I'm not quick to correct someone who is trying to affirm me. Instead, I'll let myself think about it and see if there's anything there I should pay attention to.

Affirmation does not have to be 100 percent correct to be valuable. Someone willing to affirm deserves respect and deserves to be heard. The relationship can be more important than the message.

The bottom line is: *Always be respectful toward those who affirm you.* Be respectful even when they appear to be wrong. Be respectful even if you've heard their message a thousand times before. If you show respect toward those who affirm you, you are more likely to receive the encouragement you need. You will also be doing your part to ensure that those who affirm you will also affirm others.

As you become more comfortable receiving affirmation, you must look to include affirming people in your life. Being surrounded by affirming people is as close to the Garden of Eden as we'll ever get. But these people don't usually just suddenly appear. You have to look for them and invite them into your life. You may meet them one at a time or in a group. You will find that the better you get at receiving affirmation, the more affirming people will enter your life.

As you become skilled in the art of affirmation, you will be teaching this art to others. In the process, your circle of affirming people will grow. Eventually, you will create contexts—such as families, church groups, and workplaces—where affirmation is a fundamental part of the culture. In these wonderful places, no one needs to feel guilty for saying, "I appreciate your gifts." Encouragement is *encouraged*. People thrive in these environments.

The first time I gave a workshop on affirmation something unforeseen occurred that helps make this point, something that demonstrated the power of context, specifically as it relates to affirmation. An hour or so after we began, I saw a man laughing to himself. His quiet yet obvious giggling continued until I felt I needed to address it. When I asked him what was going on, he replied, "If I went back to my job and did this stuff, I'd get laughed out of the place." (Keep in mind that this fellow *wanted* to come to this session.)

I've heard this sort of thing many times since. This man believed, perhaps correctly, that his workplace would not accept expressions of admiration. He was convinced that his work environment could not appreciate the human need for affirmation. In other words, just as there are individuals who will not receive sincere praise, there are contexts that resist it as well.

These places are terribly unhealthy yet, sadly, more prevalent than we would like to believe. While in some cases a determined individual can breathe life into these dark arenas, there are times when the healthiest choice is to leave such a place.

No group of human beings will be healthy until they are *willing* to affirm. Yet genuine affirmation is, and always will be, a *choice*. No one can be forced into it. Forced affirmation, like insincere affirmation, is weak affirmation. Many people decide not to encourage and admire. If enough of these people get together, they can create a workplace, family, or community that sabotages efforts to affirm.

Sometimes a person will have trouble giving and receiving affirmation because he lives in an environment that does not allow it. His need for encouragement will, of course, always be there. But the need is not likely to be adequately met in such a context.

Maybe that man in the workshop eventually persuaded his coworkers to become more encouraging.

Or perhaps he had to leave that company in order to find what he needed. Then there's the possibility that he continues living day to day in that toxic, stifling environment.

I can't say for sure, but I really don't think he took that third option. I don't believe he was able to stay in an unaffirming environment. You see, one of the most popular methods of avoiding affirmation is to *deny the need for it*. If we can persuade ourselves that it's not necessary, we don't have to risk giving it or opening ourselves to receive it. If we can convince ourselves that it's not that important, then we will stay in places where it is not available. And when we face those times when we would really love to hear someone say we're doing something right, we can try to dismiss it with a "but that's just me."

When we realize that it's *not just me*, that we *all* need to hear that we have something valuable to offer, we *change*. When we respect the need for affirmation—in both ourselves and others—we are less likely to surrender to communities that disregard this need.

I admire those who are willing to affirm even though they live in environments that refuse to appreciate affirmation. A single courageous, persistent soul can bring life to a stagnant situation. I also admire people virtuous enough to walk away from unhealthy places. The good people in Alcoholics Anonymous say that if you want to stay healthy you must "stick with the winners." This is not at all an elitist attitude. A *winner* may be a penniless person who lives on the street. More than anything, a winner is someone who helps you live the healthiest life possible, regardless of your status.

A winner is someone who helps bring out the best in you. It's a person who helps you make good decisions. A winner is someone who helps you become everything you were meant to be. In order to find the winners, you may have to leave where you are now. You may have to say goodbye to your workplace or your friends at the bar.

Those who have difficulty receiving affirmation will look to live in kingdoms that outlaw admiration and encouragement. They may find some shelter there, but they will never find happiness.

To find happiness, we must be willing to help each other grow. It is our responsibility to help each other find and nurture our God-given gifts. Happiness is a product of this process. In order to find happiness, we must be willing to give and receive love and encouragement.

Fortunately, it's never too late to learn the art of giving and receiving affirmation.

CHAPTER SEVEN
An Act of Love

*N*apoleon believed that the greatest discovery he ever made was that men would be willing to risk their lives for the privilege of wearing small medals on their chests.[1] We all need some kind of affirmation. We're willing to go to great lengths to receive it. Many of us are even prepared to risk our lives for it. Yet few of us feel comfortable simply asking for it.

Affirmation is often an unspoken need. It is often overlooked, too. It's not hard to convince ourselves that we're the only ones who need reassurance. As a result, we underestimate its importance. After all, how important can something be if *I* am the only one who needs it? We can miss the fact that we *all* need to be affirmed.

Affirmation is an act of love—an act of love that can be practiced between loved ones or strangers. Through this act of love, one human being helps another find and develop his or her God-given gifts. Without it, we will never become all that we were meant to be. A classroom without affirmation will be an underachieving classroom. Communities where people discourage affirmation will never reach their potential.

With each individual we encounter, we are faced with at least two questions. First: *Do I want this person to be all she can be?* If we answer this in the affirmative, then we face the second question: *Am I willing to help make this happen?*

When someone lives the art of affirmation, he tends to answer *yes* to both questions. No one can be all things to all people. We are all limited by time, energy, and resources. Still, the art of affirmation is meant to be a lifestyle. It's not so much about how we approach specific individuals; as it develops, it becomes an approach to *life*. It's a commitment to doing what we can to help others develop their gifts.

One of the beauties of affirmation is that it can be done in seconds. It does not usually require vast amounts of time or energy. It may be our most effective tool in our efforts to help people become all they can be. Affirmation involves an ability to recognize the good qualities in people and the willingness to express appreciation for these special traits. Once this practice becomes a lifestyle, we spend our lives helping others grow to become everything they should be.

You can, however, only affirm what is *real*. You cannot genuinely affirm someone just because you want to or because it seems like the polite thing to do. You cannot sincerely affirm someone for a gift that isn't there. Flattery and affirmation have little in common. Remember: those who are good in the art of affirmation make their words believable. Much of their credibility comes from the fact that they believe what they say.

Look for the good in others that has surfaced as well as the special qualities that may still be in their embryonic stage. Everyone has undeveloped potential. Affirmation is about appreciating what is real *as well as that which is becoming real*. By recognizing potential, we help make it real.

Goethe realized: "If we take man as he ought to be, we help him become it."[2] We need to look for gifts that dwell beneath the surface, the emerging—and yet to emerge—blessings that are meant to be part of a person's life. The art of affirmation is about deciding to do what you can to help people develop those blessings. At times, your contributions can only be small ones. They are contributions nonetheless. An affirming person is continually contributing.

Approaching people in an affirming way, however, need not blind you to their faults. There's little benefit in pretending that any one of us is perfect. There will always be a need for constructive criticism. Parents, teachers, friends, spouses, and employers all need to know how to offer correction. Constructive criticism is another tool used to help people become the best they can be.

Affirmation and constructive criticism often complement each other. It's easier to take criticism from someone who really appears to be rooting for you. When you know they want the best for you, you are more likely to accept what they tell you, even if it's painful at first. On the other hand, affirmation may seem more believable when it comes from someone willing to tell you an ugly truth. A person willing to point, in a pastoral way, to a flaw that needs your attention may indeed be an honest soul. Someone whose words of encouragement may feel honest, courageous, and sincere.

Affirmation and constructive criticism are both useful in helping people develop their gifts. In most relationships, however, affirmations should far outnumber criticisms. Remember, the art of affirmation begins with looking for people's *blessings*. As this skill develops you find there is usually far more to affirm in people than correct. As you get better at finding the best in others, your opportunities for affirmation will increase.

If, however, you tend to look for faults in people, your need to criticize them may surpass your willingness to admire them. You may discover the imperfections but miss the gifts. This isn't fair to you or to them, so refuse to limit yourself to this realm. Try to recognize the good in people, as well as the good that can be. Affirming a noticeable virtue may be more beneficial than criticizing a perceived vice. Strengthen the best you find in people, and they will often make the necessary corrections themselves.

A Passion for People

You tend to find affirmation, to one degree or another, in places where people *love* people. It is in greatest supply wherever people have a passion for people. Passion is love in motion. It has energy, determination, and courage. Passion is the force that turns passive into active.

Those who have a passion for people are driven to help others become the best they can be. People with this passion are bold and relentless. They don't apologize for their determination to help people grow. They have faith in the power of love. They live the conviction that it is right to encourage and admire.

This passion for people need not be loud or flamboyant (although it could be). It may be quiet, patient, and gentle. Passion is the feeling that something is so important to you that you are willing to leave your comfort zone for it. Those who have a passion for people love to encourage. They cheer a little louder, send affirmation notes when others wouldn't think to, and see gifts in people when others cannot.

Those with a passion for people continue to affirm even while surrounded by individuals who will not. Passion pushes them above conformity. It won't let them do what other people do just because other people do it. Passion demands that they live what they love.

I believe there is a passion for people in all of us. Although we may acquire a layer of insecurity and self-ishness, underneath this exterior there remains a desire to help people become their best. The human race could not survive without this passion. It drives us to sacrifice for each other. The greatest source of motivation for human beings is, and always will be, love. When we allow ourselves to love something, we come to feel a powerful need to help it grow.

In order to master the art of affirmation, you must allow your passion to surface. *You have to free the energy inside you that seeks to make ours a better world.* This is the bottom line. You can develop your eye for virtues and talents. Your methods and timing will improve, and you can grow in your understanding of human develop-ment. But it all comes together when you release your passion for people.

As you allow yourself to love, you will feel the need to affirm. Recognize this need. Be sincere and courageous, and never forget that *we all need affirmation!*

Notes

Chapter Two

1. C. W. Baars, *Born Only Once: The Miracle of Affirmation* (Quincy, IL: Franciscan Press, Quincy University, 2001), 12.

Chapter Four

1. M. Beattie, *More Language of Letting Go* (Hazelden, MN: Center City, 2000), 317.

Chapter Five

1. M. L. Jaffe, *Adolescence* (New York: John Wiley & Sons, Inc., 1998), 196.

2. C. W. Baars, *Born Only Once: The Miracle of Affirmation* (Quincy, IL: Franciscan Press, Quincy University, 2001), 25.

Chapter Seven

1. L. B. Jones, *The Path: Creating Your Mission Statement for Work and Life* (New York: Hyperion, 1996), 109.

2. In V. E. Frankl, *Psychotherapy and Existentialism* (New York: Simon and Schuster, 1967), 12.

ILLUMINATIONBOOKS

Other Books in the Series

Everyday Virtues
        by John W. Crossin, OSFS

The Mysteries of Light
        by Roland J. Faley, TOR

Healing Mysteries
        by Adrian Gibbons Koester

Carrying the Cross with Christ
        by Joseph T. Sullivan

Saintly Deacons
        by Deacon Owen F. Cumming

Finding God Today
        by E. Springs Steele

Hail Mary and Rhythmic Breathing
        by Richard Galentino

The Eucharist
        by Joseph M. Champlin

Gently Grieving
        by Constance M. Mucha

Devotions for Caregivers
        by Marilyn Driscoll

Be a Blessing
        by Elizabeth M. Nagel